THE STRANGE DEATH
OF MARXISM

THE STRANGE DEATH
OF MARXISM

The European Left in the

New Millennium

Paul Edward Gottfried

University of Missouri Press
Columbia and London

Library of Congress Cataloging-in-Publication Data

Gottfried, Paul.
    The strange death of Marxism : the European left in the new millennium /
Paul Edward Gottfried.
          p.   cm.
    Summary: "Describes a twentieth-century transformation in European
leftist and Marxist politics. European Marxism began as an economically
focused workers' movement, then became the domain of those desiring
cultural transformation of Western Europe. The transformation emphasizes
Western European guilt and promotes multiculturalism, feminism, and
acceptance of alternative lifestyles condemned by European cultures"—
Provided by publisher.
    Includes index.
    ISBN-13: 978-0-8262-1597-0 (alk. paper)
    ISBN-10: 0-8262-1597-1 (alk. paper)
    1. Communism—Europe.   2. Socialism—Europe.   I. Title.
    HX238.5.G68   2005
    320.53'15'094—dc22   2005009962

♾™ This paper meets the requirements of the
American National Standard for Permanence of Paper
for Printed Library Materials, Z39.48, 1984.

Designer: Stephanie Foley
Typesetter: Phoenix Type, Inc.
Printer and binder: Thomson-Shore, Inc.
Typeface: Plantin

CONTENTS

PREFACE

A MONG THOSE acquaintances I wish to acknowledge for reading parts or all of my text or providing research information are Drs. David Brown, David Gordon, Will Hay, James Kurth, W. Wesley McDonald, Stanley Michalak, Martha Pennington, Gabriel Ricci, Paul Craig Roberts, Wayne Selcher, and Joseph Stromberg. Two German scholars who have spared me the need to travel more extensively in search of data are Stefan Hernold and Guido Hülsmann. Their e-mail communications benefited me immensely as I was working on my many footnotes. My former colleague, Professor Emeritus Frederick Ritsch, did more than simply go through my material in earlier drafts. He also shared with me the books and reams of notes he had collected on postwar French Communism, an intricate subject that Professor Ritsch had once intended to treat in a monograph. With due acknowledgment, I have incorporated his arguments about the essentially non-Marxist character of French Communist intellectuals. A young economist, Ian Fletcher, checked the accuracy of my statistics. Where our sources diverged, I often readily deferred to his superior judgment. Finally, my colleague and, unlike me, a computer specialist Kathryn R. Kellie imposed technical consistency on my pages, which had offered a truly astonishing variety of fonts and margin spaces.

I am also indebted to my recently deceased friend Paul Piccone, longtime editor of *Telos*, for having ferociously debated with me the topics broached in this work and in the two preceding volumes on the managerial state. Although Paul might have considered me too far removed from his qualified loyalties to the Frankfurt School, I do endorse his adaptation of its critical method and have applied his insights to my work. And despite my reservations about Theodor Adorno's therapeutic politics, I have incorporated his insights into my analysis of both contemporary mechanisms of control and their ideological self-justifications.

Elizabethtown College, where I work and which is across from my house, has assisted me in many small ways, making available library staff that helped me hunt down references, scheduling a public lecture in which I could try out my notions on my hapless colleagues and students, and offering professional development funds. The Earhart Foundation has graciously funded this research, after having financed my work for the preceding twenty years. Formulations of my thesis have been printed in *Catholica, Conflits Actuels, Telos, Journal of Libertarian Studies,* and *Orbis;* all of these periodicals should be acknowledged for having granted me outlets for my ideas. Since my wife, Mary, had to endure the ordeal of listening to this work in progress, I owe her an apology as well as gratitude. In the future I shall try not to inflict on her such windy earfuls.

I am beholden for the inspiration behind this book to a former best seller, Allan Bloom's *The Closing of the American Mind.* Since I first encountered this book in 1987, the assertions of its now deceased author, a professor at the University of Chicago and a "conservative" critic of American culture and manners, have aroused in me continuing perplexity. Bloom's remarks about the "German connection" of the American academic Left seemed so far off the mark that it blew my mind that otherwise sensible commentators discussed them with approval. If such antiegalitarian German villains as Friedrich Nietzsche and Martin Heidegger had prepared the way for Nazism and the American New Left, as Bloom tells us, then these charges are far from self-evident. They have to be proved and not merely stated. So too does another related contention found in *The Closing of the American Mind,* that the driving principle of the American Left is not radical egalitarianism but ideas about particularity and historical relativism that Americans had imported from Europe.

A question that should be addressed is why those who should know better accept such opinions. Moreover, why are Europeans blamed for movements and concepts that we Americans have had the means and personnel to generate on our own? The present volume seeks to provide at least tentative answers to these questions.

THE STRANGE DEATH
OF MARXISM

INTRODUCTION

A NALYZING THE Italian municipal elections in the spring of 1999, longtime Italian political analyst Ernesto Galli della Loggia explained in the Milanese daily *Corriere della Sera* that voters were defying journalistic expectations. The working class was not voting for the Left in the numbers that had been predicted, whereas the Communists and other leftist parties were attracting a constituency consisting of gay, ecological, multicultural, and feminist activists and, more generally, of unmarried professionals. We are led to conclude that both "unconventional lifestyles" and distaste for an older European morality were characteristic of the changing Italian Left. The Italian Communists of his youth, della Loggia observes nostalgically, had well-defined goals: They backed the Soviet Union in foreign affairs, proclaimed their devotion to the class struggle, and voted for a party that called for nationalizing the means of production. But at the end of the day what these voters wanted were social benefits, to be extracted from the government and the chiefs of Italian industries *(la classe padronale)*, and, above all, the amenities of bourgeois life.[1] Least of all did working-class Communists long for the freedom to practice alternative lifestyles or hope to demasculinize the workplace.

As the author of *The French Communists,* Annie Kriegel, notes, it is hard to find any group that would have been as mystified as her

---

1. Ernesto Galli della Loggia, "Quando i ceti medi bocciano la sinistra," *Corriere della Sera,* July 4, 1999, 1.

subjects by the very notion of gender parity. Into the 1970s, membership in the party was almost 70 percent male, while women exercised only "minimal influence" over party decisions.[2] Moreover, the comments about women and family life heard at party meetings would have befitted a gathering of pre–Vatican Two Catholic prelates. Kriegel emphasizes in her study the contrast between the economic radicalism and the profoundly conservative social attitudes of the French Communists she had known. But by the 1990s the same writer was devoting her forays into journalism to denouncing the Communists and their Socialist allies, for trying to radicalize French society.[3] At issue was no longer the stodgy culture attached to French Marxism but its transmutation into a radicalizing cultural force allied to state power.

Circumstances had intervened to change the meaning of *Marxist*. European Communist parties no longer form massive working-class blocs that control, as they did in France and Italy after the Second World War, up to a third of the national vote. Indeed membership in European working-class unions fell dramatically throughout the nineties, a trend taken up in a feature investigation in *Le Monde Diplomatique*. The author of the study, Pierre Bordieu, worries that organized workers would soon be insufficiently noticeable to influence French government attitudes. On the economic front, policy differences between the Right and Left have narrowed down to mere detail. The Right accepts and even expands the welfare state, while the Left has scuttled plans for government control of industries. Talk about a "third way" between capitalism and socialism has replaced the radical Left's appeal to class conflict; meanwhile left-of-center governments in Germany, France, and England trim public budgets as well as redistribute incomes.[4] Most importantly, the once muscular Communist vote machines are now picking up only enough support (between 5 and 8 percent)

2. Annie Kriegel, *The French Communists: Profile of a People*, trans. Elaine P. Halperin (Chicago: University of Chicago Press, 1994), 61–64.

3. Annie Kriegel, "Sur l'antifascisme," *Commentaire* 12 (summer 1990), 299; see also Kriegel's autobiography, *Ce que j'ai cru comprendre* (Paris: Robert Laffont, 1991), which applies the perspective of a disenchanted Communist to the ideological changes undergone by the French Communist Party since the postwar years.

4. Pierre Bordieu, "Pour un mouvement européen," *Le Monde Diplomatique*, June 2, 1999, 16.

to help fill out the left-of-center coalitions in Italy and France—or in the German case to offer the SPD an alternative partner to the Greens. The first round of the French presidential race on April 21, 2003, ended in a debacle for the Communist Party. In a race that saw the candidate of the populist Right Jean-Marie Le Pen finish second, the Communist candidate (and Communist party chief) Robert Hué came in fifth, with only 3 percent of the vote. Being ineligible for matching funds for the 8 million Euros spent on the disastrous campaign, after failing to reach the 5 percent eligibility level, the party had to put its own headquarters up for sale to get out of arrears.[5]

Today European CPs survive merely as adjuncts of larger concentrations of power on the Left. Whatever the chief cause for this development, whether a general rise in living standards, a disintegrating working-class solidarity, or the demonstrated unattractiveness of Communist practice, Communist parties in Western Europe have lost their electoral appeal. Although they occasionally do stage comebacks in Poland, Hungary, Russia, or the Baltic states, this may be happening because of populations spooked by an overly abrupt transition to a free or quasi-free market economy. It would in any case be hard to prove that the sporadic electoral successes of renamed Communist parties in Eastern Europe indicate a renewed belief in either Marxism or in working-class cohesion.

Among conservative critics, it has been customary to explain this retooling of nominal Communists as junior partners of the Center-Left in one or more of several ways. The boosters of an American foreign policy based on global democracy, for example, Michael Novak of the American Enterprise Institute, Francis Fukuyama, and George Gilder, maintain that American "democratic capitalism" has become well-nigh irresistible; thus onetime European Marxists are running to embrace "the American model," combining a welfare state with growing possibilities for capital investment. Everyone but the most benighted has adopted this middle road between a pure free market and a state-run economy, which

5. See Marie-Claire Lavabie and François Platone, *Que reste-il du PCF?* (Paris: Editions Autrement, 2003), 66–73; and Bernard Dolez and Annie Laurent, "Marches et marges de la gauche," in Pascal Perrineau and Colette Ysmal, *Le vote de tous les refus* (Paris: Presses de Sciences-Po, 2003).

reconciles the demand for human equality with material incentives and material progress.[6]

Less sanguine observers on the more traditional Right, however, have questioned whether the Communist predator has really been declawed. And some of the doubts raised merit attention. All European parliamentary coalitions that include Communists avoid the recognition of the mass murder committed by Communist regimes in Russia and elsewhere. Such fits of denial were in evidence in the French National Assembly on November 12, 1997, and then, on January 27, 2000, in the Italian assembly. On the first occasion, French Socialist prime minister Lionel Jospin, responding to a question from the opposition about whether he believed that Stalin had killed millions of people, fell back, partly out of deference to his Communist coalition partner, into syntactical evasion. Jospin insisted that "the Communist Revolution was one of the great events of our century," and "whatever judgment one cares to make about Stalin's Russia, it was our ally against Nazi Germany." And while there was a "tragic" aspect attached to Soviet history, the prime minister considered it "intrinsically perverse to assign equal blame to Communism and Nazism."[7] So much for facing up to the genocidal equivalence between Nazi and Communist mass murderers, while tending to political allies whom Jospin was "proud to be affiliated with."

Equally revealing of the Stalinist legacy of the European Left were the negotiations for a proposal put forth by the left-of-center (then ruling) coalition in Italy, to declare a yearly "day of remembrance for fascist-Nazi crimes." When a member of the center-right opposition proposed to widen this commemoration to "all victims of political tyranny," the other side pointedly refused. One Communist deputy complained that the "continuing obsession" with things that may or may not have happened under Commu-

6. See Michael Novak, *The Spirit of Democratic Capitalism* (New York: Simon and Schuster, 1982); George Gilder, *The Spirit of Enterprise* (New York: Simon and Schuster, 1984); and Francis Fukuyama, "The End of History?" *National Interest* 16 (summer 1989), 4–6.

7. *Le Monde*, November 14, 1997, 8. For a less admiring description of this confrontation, see Jean Sévillia, *Le terrorisme intellectuel: De 1945 à nos jours* (Paris: Perrin, 2000), 202–4.

nist governments was only a cover-up. What the Center-Right was really doing was "not coming to terms with its participation in the fascist legislation of 1938 [stripping Italian Jews of citizenship] or in the subsequent deportation of Jews [in 1943]."[8] In point of fact there is no one in the present Center-Right who could have been implicated in either misdeed, the second of which was done by the SS and by a small percentage of the Italian population.[9] There is also nothing to justify a comparison between the present Italian parliamentary Center-Right and the fascist government of the late thirties or, even less, with the Salo Republic that the German occupation imposed on Italy in 1943. Unlike the Italian Center-Left, moreover, the Italian Center-Right would not hesitate to repudiate all totalitarianism. For those who link the old and new Communists, this adamant refusal to come to terms with the Communist past and the dismissal of any attempt to concede its misdeeds as "fascist" both demonstrate the obvious.

One can also cite the recycling of the East German Communists and their West German sympathizers as the Party of Democratic Socialists, established in the nineties, as a further bridge between the Communist past and present. The former party leader, Gregor Gysi, was a documented Stasi agent, who after the fall of the Berlin Wall worked to organize "antifascist" rallies in the reunited Berlin. His career as an informer for the Communist secret police, between 1975 and 1987, came to light in 1995, after the German Bundestag had issued an amnesty to Gysi upon receiving a confirmed report about his activities as a Stasi spy. When his Christian Democratic opposition played up this connection, the leftist press in Germany and Austria accused Gysi's opponents of engaging in a witch hunt. His chief rival in Berlin, Frank Steffel, backed down after leading German journalists had knocked him around as an unforgiving anti-Communist fanatic. The subdued Steffel agreed never again to mention Gysi's work in handing over those

8. For an account of this Italian parliamentary discussion, see *Il Mattino*, April 17, 2000, 17.

9. For less severe pictures of Mussolinian anti-Semitism after as well as before 1938, see Léon Poliakov, *Gli ebrei sotto l'occupazione italiana* (Milan: Comunità, 1956); Meir Michaelis, *Mussolini and the Jews* (Oxford: Clarendon Press, 1978); and Renzo De Felice, *Storia degli ebrei sotto il fascismo* (Turin: Einaudi, 1977).

whose confidence he had betrayed to the East German Communist regime.[10]

But there is nothing exceptional about this immunity that the media has issued to someone who had sojourned on the radical Left. Despite his proximity to the violence-prone Left in the 1960s, German foreign minister Joschka Fischer has not taken flak from the mainstream German press. And the same has been true for how the press in France treats dismissively the lengthy association of Jospin with a militant Trotskyist faction. In 1991, longtime Communist activist Georges Boudarel was brought before a criminal court in France for assisting in the death of French detainees in 1953, who had been rounded up by the Communist Vietminh during their guerrilla war in Indochina with the French. Unlike the arrest of suspected Nazi collaborators from World War II, this politically incorrect attempt to settle accounts with an accomplice in mass murder inflamed the Paris press. Those who brought charges, among the few living survivors of the Vietminh Camp 113, were attacked as "objective allies of [Holocaust] revisionism" seeking to "banalize Nazism."[11] Boudarel was released on a technicality, which did not touch the substance of the charges, but by then mass demonstrations were being planned on the Paris Left Bank against this supposed victim of Nazi "*collabos.*"

Noting the media portrayal of such incidents, French journalist and onetime advisor of Charles de Gaulle, Maurice Druon, views the political history of France since the end of World War II as overshadowed by the Communists and their hangers-on.[12] According to Druon, a steady kowtowing to the totalitarian Left continues to take place although the CP has dwindled in members. Politicians go on about "fascism" out of habit and because they still cannot grasp how weak Communism has become as an electoral force. They also fear reprisals from pro-Communist journalists, who interpret any notice given to the seamy side of the Communist past as proof of fascist inclinations.

Druon is right to note certain behavioral quirks on the French

10. See the commentaries on this relation in Berlin politics in *Junge Freiheit*, July 13, 2001, and July 27, 2001.

11. *Libération*, November 11, 1997, 1–4; Sévillia, *Le terrorisme*, 204–5.

12. Maurice Druon, *La France aux ordres d'un cadavre* (Paris: Fallois/Rocher, 2001).

left. The grotesque rhetoric that Jospin deployed to jolly up the Communists, which François Mitterrand had expressed before him, confirms Druon's charge, that some French politicians will do anything to curry Communist favor. But it might be fitting to ask whether the Communists and their sympathizers are indeed Marxists or Marxist-Leninists. Do Communists, for example, still teach a dialectical materialist view of history, culminating in a workers' revolution and in a socialist society predicated on public ownership of the means of production? In what sense do Communists believe in class struggle as the key to grasping human relations and as the vehicle by which socialism might be brought into being? Note that for serious Communists what is bad about "fascism" is not that it opposes immigration (which in fact fascists never worried about) or that it encourages insensitive speech against Third World minorities. Fascists, in traditional Communist teachings, are engaged in a struggle against the working class and join with beleaguered capitalists to stave off a socialist revolution. In short, fascists are seen as a class enemy, who are trying to frustrate the historical process and to reverse the material dynamics leading to the predestined end of all class conflict, a postcapitalist workers' society that Communist organizers will be in a position to establish.

Such basic Communist ideas, which were widely diffused in the 1930s, when there were fascists on the hoof, have little to do with the current European Left. The reason may be that the Left is no longer Marxist and only intermittently socialist. Looking at the legislation Communists have pushed center-left coalitions into supporting—from hate-speech laws directed primarily against the European Christian majority populations, through the criminalization of published or televised communications deemed to deny or minimize Nazi acts of genocide, to the sponsoring of multicultural programs, the declaration of national commemorations for the deportation of Nazi victims, gay rights, and the raising of public subsidies for asylum-seekers—it is not clear how these projects fit into Marxist revolution. His electoral success did not lead Gregor Gysi, an ex-Communist spy, into bringing East German Communism westward.[13] He and other longtime Communist

13. Gysi's autobiography, published after he had stepped down from his leadership role in the PDS in the wake of revelations about his prolonged cooperation

partisans built up the Party of German Socialists around a different agenda, namely, government-protection of gay rights, the loosening of restrictions on German "asylum-seekers," and preferential immigration for Third World *Zuwanderer,* at the expense of ethnic Germans who wish to resettle in Germany from the former Soviet Union. Gysi's party entered the municipal government of Berlin, in alliance with the German Socialist Party and Berlin's Socialist mayor, Klaus Wowereit, a homosexual activist whose politics do not seem to be Marxist, despite the fact that he and his coalition partners have supported the building of a monument to the Marxist revolutionary Rosa Luxemburg, involved in the abortive Spartacist uprising of 1919. This choice of heroines fits to a T the socially radical politics of Gysi and Wowereit. A Polish-Jewish leftist revolutionary, Luxemburg attempted to overthrow the infant German Weimar Republic and was slain by military officers who allegedly expressed anti-Semitic sentiments after killing her. Luxemburg was known to have criticized Lenin, who she believed had failed to carry out a proper Marxist revolution. Lenin, according to this gloss, had distorted the revolutionary act by putting in charge a party vanguard. Thus there arose a perfect symbol of the post-Communist Left, a Jewish victim destroyed by reactionary Germans while upholding a model revolutionary vision. But does this glorification of a foreign revolutionary "victim" express Marxism or any traditional Communist program?[14]

A response to this query has come from critics of "cultural Marxism," and most explicitly, from Pat Buchanan in *The Death of the West,* a work that depicts the attack on "bourgeois morality," launched by German émigrés of the Frankfurt School, as a new and dangerous phase of the Marxist war against Western Christian

---

with the East German secret police, spells out his "antifascist" stance. He defends the East German Communists on the grounds that, unlike the West German republic, they were serious about hunting down and punishing Nazis and eradicating German nationalism. Gysi also plays up the fact that he had Jewish ancestors, which serves to link him psychologically to victims of the Holocaust. See Gregor Gysi, *Ein Blick zurück: Ein Schritt nach vorn* (Hamburg: Hoffmann und Campe Verlag, 2001).

14. Wowereit lists on his website "the placing of a monument to Rosa Luxemburg on the square named for her" as one of the "guidelines" of his administration, together with the construction of separate memorials to gypsy and homosexual victims of fascism; see www.klaus.wowereit.de.regierensrichtlinien.htm.

society. According to Buchanan, Theodor Adorno, Max Hork-heimer, Herbert Marcuse, and Eric Fromm were all German social radicals who rebuilt Marxism from an economic doctrine into a morally subversive force.[15] Buchanan focuses on *The Authoritarian Personality,* a collection of critical essays edited by Adorno and Horkheimer that came out in 1950. In this ponderous indictment of "bourgeois Christian" society, traditional bourgeois values are made to seem "pathological" and "pre-fascist." Through its "critical theory" applied to the established culture, the Frankfurt School, which moved to the United States from Germany in the 1930s, laid the base for its reconstructed Marxist revolution. In this new formulation, socialists would be concerned less with economic exploitation than with vicious prejudice and its seemingly respectable bearers. Unless removed from power, the dominant class would go on engendering racial hatred, anti-Semitism, misogyny, and homophobia. Cataclysmic change was essential to get rid of bourgeois society, which the Frankfurt School maintained was a source of social pathology.

The presentation of cultural Marxism as the post-Communist Left may be the most plausible attempt to find a doubtful Marxist continuity. It takes seriously the claim that Frankfurt School theorists make for themselves as "Marxist cultural critics." As a former student of Herbert Marcuse, I can personally testify that this cultural Marxist never doubted that he was vindicating Marxist-Leninist tenets. Marcuse found nothing dissimilar thematically between his observations in *One-Dimensional Man,* about the erotic restrictions of bourgeois culture, and Marx's dialectical materialism. Both were attempts to highlight the "irrational" nature of capitalist society reflected in its incapacity to satisfy human wants. Moreover, Marcuse had praise for Soviet Russian socialism and, like another Frankfurt School groupie, Georg Lukacs, went out of his way to defend the Soviet "assault on fascism," when Soviet tanks crushed the Hungarian "socialist" uprising in 1956.[16] Marcuse combined devotion to Marxist-Leninism, in its Stalinist form, with postbourgeois erotic fantasy. But no necessary connection

15. Patrick J. Buchanan, *The Death of the West* (New York: St. Martin's Press, 2002), 78–92.

16. For a devastating attack on Marcuse's politics by another mentor of mine, see Eliseo Vivas, *Contra Marcuse* (New Rochelle: Arlington House, 1974).

existed between the two, other than the fact that Marx had predicted the end of bourgeois society followed by workers' socialism.

Nothing intrinsically Marxist, that is to say, defines "cultural Marxism," save for the evocation or hope of a postbourgeois society. Those who advocate this new Marxism, however, are driven not by historical materialism but by revulsion for bourgeois Christian civilization. The mistake of those who see one position segueing into another is to confuse contents with personalities. For example, the late Bella Abzug, who was descended from a family of Russian Jewish radicals, began her political career as a Communist who denounced the American government for arming England during the period of the Soviet-Nazi Pact. Abzug later became an outspoken feminist, who by the end of her life was championing gay issues. But while this self-styled rebel spent her career inside and outside of Congress on the left, it is not clear that her feminism or gay rights advocacy flowed out of her Marxist or Stalinist loyalties. Such commitments might have derived from her self-image as a marginalized Jew cast into a hostile culture. All the same, her series of positions while on the "left" do not show theoretical unity. Unlike Abzug, Marx and Lenin disliked the bourgeoisie as oppressive capitalists but did not reproach them for failing to address feminist and gay issues. The triumphant Soviets did consider abolishing marriage as a "bourgeois institution," but quickly reconsidered and finished, like later Communist regimes, by imposing a puritanical morality. Today antibourgeois social planners, like the descendants of the Frankfurt School, call themselves Marxists and parade under red banners, but they are playing with names and symbols. Such proponents represent historical and theoretical Marxism in about the same way that "liberal" Episcopal Bishop Spong of Newark is now fighting for Christian dogmatic theology.

What the critics of cultural Marxism correctly observe is that the Frankfurt School accumulated American devotees, but here further clarification may be necessary. Essential for tracing cultural Marxism's Americanization is *The Authoritarian Personality*, a dense anthology that appeared as the first of a widely advertised series, *Studies in Prejudice*. The sponsors, who approached the exiled German radicals and paid heavily for their contributions, belonged to the very nonradical American Jewish Committee. At the time

that *The Authoritarian Personality* was coming out, the same bene-
factors were launching *Commentary* magazine, a progressive, philo-
Semitic but also anti-Soviet publication. According to Christopher
Lasch, these converging circumstances have much to teach. *The
Authoritarian Personality*'s sponsors were certainly not promoting
anti-Americanism. Whatever the residual Stalinist fixations may
have been that animated its editors, those who subsidized them
were pushing anti-Communist American patriotism, a point documented abundantly in my book *After Liberalism*. An enthusiastic
commentator and a contributor to *The Studies in Prejudice*, Seymour Martin Lipset, thought that the psychological approach to
"prejudice," particularly to anti-Semitism, featured by Adorno
and Horkheimer was a breakthrough in both sociology and the
modification of social behavior. In 1955, Lipset presented *his* adaptation of their work, a paper on "working-class authoritarianism,"
delivered before the anti-Communist, social democratic Congress
for Cultural Freedom.[17] The one puzzling problem with *The
Authoritarian Personality*, for Lipset, was the editors' "oversight"
in not including Communists among those with morbid psychic
traits. Lipset and other progressive advocates of "American democracy," however, never doubted that Adorno and Horkheimer were
prescribing sound medicine to save America from undemocratic
defects.

If "cultural Marxism" was an import into American life, it was,
like Christmas trees and hot dogs, one that flourished in its new
environment. The attempt to treat it as alien ignores certain facts.
By the time *The Authoritarian Personality* was brought to Europe,
its themes had assumed American New Left and Cold War liberal
forms. What made its psychological understanding of reactionary
attitudes so thoroughly American was the consolidation of an
American centralized administrative state, coming simultaneously
with the influx of different nationalities. The festering presence of
a "race problem" also contributed to the acceptance in the American polity of benign, scientific administration, which was supposed

17. Christopher Lasch, *The True and Only Heaven: Progress and Its Critics*
(New York: Norton, 1991), 457–61; Paul Gottfried, *After Liberalism: Mass Democracy in the Managerial State* (Princeton: Princeton University Press, 1999), 72–
109. Lipset's famous text on working-class authoritarianism appeared first in
print in the *American Sociological Review* 24 (1959), 482–501.

to solve intergroup relations by giving them a new foundation. It was the growing diversity of a changing American society, which lacked the firm ethnic character of European states, that made administered democracy, and its child, social engineering, essential to the new political landscape. The plan to secularize and sensitize Americans that radical émigrés were advancing fitted, with some modification, into what Americans were doing to and for themselves. It also in no way contradicted what mainline Protestant denominations were by then preaching about pluralism and social justice. Complaints about Protestant theology deteriorating into sentimental talk about "humanity" stretch at least as far back as the New Humanism, a circle of high-toned Yankee academics that developed in the early twentieth century. Critics of humanitarian religion Irving Babbitt and Paul Elmer More testify to the possibility that American Protestantism may now be aping its own platitudinous past.[18]

Arguably the Post-Marxist Left in Europe has borrowed heavily from American political culture. Contrary to the opinion that ideological fevers only move across the Atlantic in a westerly direction, the opposite may be closer to the truth. American books are more likely to sell in Europe than vice versa; and European televisions and theaters feature made-in-America products nonstop. After World War II, it was the United States that reconstructed German "civic culture"; it was not Europeans who conquered Americans and undertook a civilizing mission here. Nor are Americans as likely to go to Europe to study, because of linguistic laziness but also because of financial opportunities, as Europeans are likely to come to the United States. It is both anachronistic and naive to insist that Europeans cannot import their political values from here, particularly given the traumatic breaks in European life caused by the devastating wars of the last century.

This process of absorption on the European left has gone far enough to entail the introduction of policies that seem designed

18. An unsurpassed study on the religious and literary roots and political implications of American sentimentality is Irving Babbitt's *Democracy and Leadership* (1924; reprint, Indianapolis: Liberty Classics, 1991). A commentary in the same spirit, "On American Empire," by Claes Ryn, is featured in *Orbis* 47, no. 3 (summer 2003), 383–97.

for American historical situations. It is not enough that Europeans translate and imbibe American feminist authors such as Catherine MacKinnon, Andrea Dworkin, and Gloria Steinem, whose books one encounters in European capitals and who are cited in the European press. Nor is it merely the fact that European gay-libbers sound like their American counterparts in translation. Even more startling are the efforts made by European progressives to extend copies of American civil rights legislation to Third World immigrants whom Europeans had not enslaved—and who arrived in European countries of their own volition. Studies of such trends by Ray Honeyford, John Laughland, and Eric Werner drive home the extent of this mimesis when Europeans introduce "positive discrimination" for North African or West Indian immigrants, and when the popular press in Europe persist in presenting Third World populations that chose to live in Europe in the same terms that American liberals reserve for American blacks.[19] In fact, the European Left, like the Canadian and Australian Left, pushes even further the trends adapted from American sources: It insists on criminalizing politically incorrect speech as an incitement to "fascist" excess. Without the classical liberal restraints that still operate within American borders, European advocates of sensitivity demand and enforce draconian measures against insensitive white male Christians. But this points back equally to American inspiration and to such esteemed American exponents of differential free-speech rights as MacKinnon, Stanley Fish, and Cornell West. While German-born Marcuse had thundered in the sixties and seventies against the perils of "repressive tolerance," he carried on his defense of censorship from an American academic base, writing in English.

But European leftists have not become ersatz Americans without a certain perceptible ambivalence. In an Oedipal fashion, they

19. See, for example, Ray Honeyford, *The Commission for Racial Equality: British Bureaucracy and the Multiethnic Society* (New Brunswick, N.J.: Transaction Publishers, 1998), especially 51–91; John Laughland, *The Tainted Source: The Undemocratic Origins of the European Idea* (London: Trafalgar Square, 2000); Eric Werner (with Jan Marejko), *L'après-démocratie* (Lausanne, Switzerland: L'Age d'Homme, 2001); and Werner's review of my book *Multiculturalism and the Politics of Guilt*, in *Catholica* 78 (winter 2002–2003), 116–20.

have lashed out at the culture and society they imitate. Thus the European Left looks for issues that can help distinguish it from the transatlantic giant; and the farther leftward on the European spectrum one looks, the more venomous the voices become. Americans are accused of soiling the environment, dumping commodities on Third World countries to inhibit their economic growth, and siding with Israelis, depicted as Western colonialists, against Third World Palestinians. What makes these confrontations so acrimonious is their evidence of cultural dependence, that is to say, the European Left has become parasitic on American fashions. It does not any longer export anything of cultural significance to the New World, save for postmodernist literary criticism, which is an acquired taste among Ivy League English departments and their provincial satellites. In a real sense, the European Left has never recovered from the fall of the Soviet empire. While that dictatorship lumbered on, the Left could claim association with a Marxist tradition linked to a world military power and could point to an idealized Soviet Union while confronting American consumerism and cultural vulgarity.[20] With the disintegration of the Communist bloc, a full-blown socialist world state was gone. Meanwhile a widening American influence made sure that European leftists would combine their nostalgia for Communist dictatorships with American fads. Whence the current hybrid Left that prevails in Europe and calls for policies that might originate with an American social worker or with an American academic feminist.

A final point concerns a hypothesis that is being ruled out, namely that Americans, Canadians, and Western Europeans have discovered the same ideological issues simultaneously. Since these peoples had undergone parallel processes, for example, a transition from a late industrial to a service economy or the transfer of female labor from domestic to wage-earning employment, conceivably they could have arrived at the same ideas together. But this conclusion

---

20. The argument about the Soviets' role in providing an alternative paradigm to the American empire, particularly for French Communists, is in Stéphane Courtois and Marc Lazar, *Histoire du parti communiste*, 2d ed. (Paris: Presses Universitaires de France, 2000); Marc Lazar, *Le communisme: Une passion française* (Paris: Perrin, 2002); and Michel Dreyfus, *Le siècle des communismes* (Paris: Edition de l'Atelier, 2000).

must be challenged. One can point to economically advanced societies in which women have entered the workforce in large numbers, for example, in Japan, but in which feminism, gay liberation, and multiculturalism have had relatively little impact.

Although in Italy one finds many of the same trends in family life as one does in Germany—low birth rate and women entering careers—the ideological changes have not been equally dramatic in both societies. In Germany one encounters a much larger and far more vocal feminist movement than one does in Italy. It is countries and groups with predisposing features that reveal the strongest propensity for American political culture: for example, the Germans, who have ostentatiously rejected their historical traditions, or Anglophone societies, which are drawn into the American political-cultural orbit as junior partners. Finally, given the vast disparity in who receives what from whom, it is unlikely that Europeans have not been heavily influenced by their American cousins. The United States exports its cultural products to Europeans relative to what it takes back at a rate of fifty to one. Ben Wattenberg, in *The First Universal Nation,* cites this fact as evidence of American cultural superiority.[21] But looking beyond the intent of Wattenberg's judgment, it is possible to conclude with less American chauvinism that cultural commerce is useful for indicating influence. The simultaneous-development approach to ideology may not be applicable when the influences being studied are going largely in one direction.

It may also be necessary to raise questions about a school of social criticism, exemplified by Allan Bloom's *Closing of the American Mind,* that make the dubious assumption that American universities and American cultural institutions have become captive to noxious foreigners, usually speaking with German accents. Such accusations appeal to American patriots who find it hard to imagine that what they find repulsive could be indigenously American.[22]

21. Ben Wattenberg, *The First Universal Nation: Leading Indicators and Ideas about the Surge of America in the 1990s* (New York: Free Press, 1991), 210–13.

22. Allan Bloom, *The Closing of the American Mind* (New York: Simon and Schuster, 1987); see also my response to Bloom's *dossier à charge* against Teutonic pollutants, Paul Gottfried, "Postmodernism and Academic Discontents," *Academic Questions* 9, no. 3 (summer 1996), 58–67.

But what the foreign-contamination school stresses is both impressionistic and emotive. Why should one believe that egalitarianism or the sentimental concern with presumed victims that permeates our academic life had to be brought from Europe before it could establish itself here? In Bloom's interpretation, it is not radical egalitarians but a "German connection," going back to Nietzsche and Heidegger, that is destroying America's moral fiber. Dead reactionary Teutons are held up to judgment as the postmodernist creators of a corrosive skepticism about American democracy and equality that Bloom fears has overtaken our universities.

Although *The Closing of the American Mind* is the Cold War liberal counterpart to Buchanan's conservative brief against foreign polluters, Bloom's interpretation offers even thinner pickings when it comes to text proofs. One leaves his book with opinions—but little else. Common to his work and Buchanan's, however, is the notion that the American empire is an oversized sponge that is indiscriminately soaking up non-American thought. By now this picture may be ready for the attic, along with other frayed objets d'art.

Chapter 2 will deal with the problematic history of Marxist theory since the 1960s, resulting from the bad fit between Marxist and Marxist-Leninist predictions and an increasingly uncooperative reality. Since advanced capitalist countries had failed to collapse under their supposed economic contradictions, since self-proclaimed Marxist governments were beset by material dearth and badly performing economies, and since the electoral strength of Western European Communist parties had peaked at, without being able to exceed, about one-third of the popular vote, it became necessary for Communists and Communist sympathizers to explain (away) these untoward situations. The resulting explanations, which came from inside and outside Communist parties, required a shift in interpretive emphasis from older Eurocentric interests. Henceforth, as remarked by historian Klaus von Beyme, theoretical Marxists would treat socialist and capitalist societies as incommensurable entities.[23] The true Marxist revolution was seen as

---

23. See Klaus von Beyme, "Vom Neomarxismus zum Post-Marxismus," *Zeitschrift für Politik* 38, no. 2 (1991), 124; and Klaus von Beyme, *Ökonomie und Politik im Sozialismus* (Munich: Piper Verlag, 1975), especially 15–19.

taking place in struggling Third World countries, such as Maoist China and Castroite Cuba; it was the preferred instrument of poor and exploited countries, which, having battled against imperialism, were now catching up to their sometime exploiters. Owing to unequal developmental positions, however, it was considered unseemly to compare those agonized Third World societies that were embracing Marxism to the First World. Besides, went this Neo-Marxist special pleading, Western capitalist societies were themselves on the verge of a shattering crisis, though the crisis, noted particularly by West German Marxists, had less to do with class conflict than it did with cutbacks in social programs. A plethora of socialist tracts published around 1970, one bearing the portentous title *Krise des Steuerstaates,* maintain that the reduction of social budgets betrays a "crisis of rationality" about to overwhelm Western societies. This crisis points back to the failure to generate enough revenue to protect workers and the unemployed and will supposedly bring about a significant modification of the socio-economic system. While social planning advocates have continued to make such statements about failing welfare states, their predictions have not had the effect of placing classical Marxist theory back on its feet. Such manufacturers of gloom and doom have not rendered more credible either the historical materialism or the vision of revolutionary socialist change that Marx and Lenin had considered essential for their work.

A second attempt to revive classical Marxism occurred in France, where Louis Althusser (1918–1990), a CP member since 1948, devised a consciously "antihumanistic" reading of Marx that sought to be consistent with the Leninist formulation.[24] In such studies as *Pour Marx* and *Lire le Capital,* both produced in the sixties, Althusser warned against the pseudo-Marxist "humanists," who denied the scientific, materialist core of Marxist teachings. The French press showered praise on the conceptual toughness of this allegedly un-French approach to Marxism, and *Pour Marx* went through numerous printings and foreign translations and sold in its French edition over forty-five thousand copies. Despite

24. See the biographical notes on Althusser by Etienne Balibar prepared as annexes to *Ecrits pour Althusser* (Paris: La Découverte, 1991) and to Althusser, *Pour Marx* (Paris: La Découverte, 1986).

the publishing success, it is difficult to think of any "revolutionary practice" prompted by this rereading of Marx or its accompanying tributes to Lenin and Mao. It may speak volumes that Althusser, before descending into madness and strangling his wife in 1980, was perpetually on the outs with the French Communist Party. Its official philosopher, Roger Garaudy, condemned his "theoretical anti-humanism" at a meeting of French Communist thinkers in 1966, and almost all of Althusser's work was published in non-Communist French journals or by Eastern European Communist governments.[25] Curiously, the outsider Althusser became hooked on psychoanalysis through another Party maverick, the sexual experimenter Michel Foucault. Despite his Communist voting habits, Foucault epitomized what Althusser claimed to despise most, the reduction of revolutionary radicalism to antibourgeois moralizing.

By the sixties, Chapters 2 and 3 will try to document, the reconfiguring of Marxist theory had strayed into alien territory. By elevating psychology and culture into the key for understanding historical conditions, Neo-Marxists would abandon the older materialist paradigm, into which Althusser had tried to breathe new life. His disciple and editor Etienne Balibar illustrates the extent of the straying that occurred. Balibar moved away from an "anti-humanistic" Marxism to a discovery of his Jewish roots mingled with Spinoza's ethics. By the nineties he had branched out into "antifascist" activities by working for a multicultural European society that would treat European national identities as an altogether unfortunate but dispensable legacy.[26]

Others took equally tortuous paths away from Marxist Leninism, while believing themselves to have remained on the same revolutionary course. Neo-Hegelians who had been drawn to

25. See Balibar's biographical notes to *Pour Marx*, 271–73. According to Philippe Robrieux's *Histoire intérieure du parti communiste, 1972–1982*, vol. 3 (Paris: Fayard, 1982), 112–16, the midseventies, when the Party turned against Althusser "for ignoring its collective reflections," coincided with a sharp erosion of Communist electoral support and the beginning of a generally fruitless alliance with the Socialist Party. The imposition of increased thought control was the central committee's initial reaction to this downward trend.

26. See Balibar, *Spinoza et la politique* (Paris: Presses Universitaires de France, 1985); and Balibar, *Les frontières, l'état, le peuple* (Paris: La Découverte, 2001).

Marxism, like the Italian Communist Antonio Gramsci, found their own ways of breaking with an apparently exhausted materialist view. By focusing on the cultural preconditions for capitalism and socialism, Gramsci was able to change the dialectical materialist conversation to reactionary hegemonic cultures. And Foucault's *L'histoire de la folie* (1961) gave to this culturally oriented "Marxist" critique a particularly sharp thrust by presenting the concept of mental illness as a form of social repression. Mental asylums were set up, according to Foucault, to deal with dissidence and protest while pretending to treat the sick.[27] Perhaps best illustrating of this turn toward an alternative Marxism was the activity of the Frankfurt School, which carried out its own transposition of Marxist concepts and symbols. Frankfurt School theorists demonized those whom Marx and Lenin had defined as class enemies by depicting them as insensitive bigots. In this recasting of a received revolutionary doctrine, the class enemy would be those guilty of prejudice and sexual repression.

Chapter 4 will focus on this overlap between the Post-Marxist Left and an evolving American political culture. A harbinger of this development was the publication in 1970 of *Ni Jésus ni Marx* by the former French Communist Jean-François Revel.[28] Although an Atlanticist tradition could be found on the European Center-Left, rooted in the Cold War, what Revel and his followers did was link Americanism to a global leftist vision. The United States was no longer to be viewed as a shield against Soviet aggression but the personification of a humane order bottomed on equality and material affluence. Revel associated this vision with a rising generation that had given up on both Christianity and Marxism (whence his title). The position expounded was intended to witness to Revel's spiritual odyssey, as someone who had left behind

27. See Michel Foucault, *L'histoire de la folie à l'âge classique* (Paris: Gallimard, 1970); and James Miller, *The Passion of Michel Foucault* (New York: Simon and Schuster, 1993).

28. Jean-François Revel, *Ni Jésus ni Marx: La nouvelle révolution mondiale a commencé aux E-U* (Paris: Laffont, 1970). For an incisive commentary on this realignment of "progressive" European opinion on the American side, viewed as the guardian of social modernization, see Jens Jessen, "Grenzschützer des Westens," *Die Zeit*, September 26, 2002, and Karlheinz Weissmann, "Querfront gegen den Westen," *Junge Freiheit*, October 11, 2002, 22.

his experiences as a Communist journalist and Communist party member. Revel looked forward to a "nuclear-free" future, in which destructive weapons would be eliminated, but such a hope could be fulfilled, the reader is left to gather, only in the shadow of a redemptive American presence. For Revel, the United States, not Europe, was henceforth the center of world history.

In the nineties the German "democratic Left" had also come to reassess its relation to the only superpower. Despite the bumpy Cold War era and disagreements on global warming, the war on Saddam Hussein and the Arab-Israeli conflict, Germanophone leftists would find aspects of American politics and society they wished to import into their own country. Generous immigration policies, a culturally pluralistic, creedal basis for citizenship, and the readiness to employ government to banish prejudice were American trends that the European Left, particularly after the collapse of the Soviet model, ran to espouse. In Germany and Austria, the Left, and more generally antinationalist Germans, regard May 8, 1945, as a *Befreiungstag*, a day of liberation instead of the beginning of a foreign occupation. Although the Soviets inflicted this celebration on the East Germans once having conquered them, today this festive occasion is meant to dramatize the benefits of the American occupation as well as the end of Nazi rule. Since the end of the Cold War, the most respected Frankfurt School spokesman, Jürgen Habermas (1929–) has been generally an outspoken supporter of the United States. During the Serbian conflict in 1999, Habermas called for an extension of American power and influence in Europe, "to bring about the cosmopolitan understanding of right that accompanies being a citizen of the world" and to crush what remained in his homeland of "nationalist sentiment."[29] The true liberation, glorified by Habermas and other despisers of the German past, was having the Americans "reeducate" them, so that they might cease to be Germans and become "democrats."

Chapter 4 will also explore the Post-Marxist ideology that has taken over the European Left. From the new European Commu-

---

29. Jürgen Habermas, *Die Moderne: Ein unvollendetes Projekt*, 3d ed. (Leipzig: Reclam Verlag, 1994), 75–85.

nist Party programs, which stress behavior modification and multi-culturalism, to the war waged by European intellectuals against prejudice, it is possible to trace a process of Americanization on the European left. Some reasons for this process are political-historical, namely, American dominance in Europe, the collapse of the Soviet empire, and the intentional reshaping of German society by American conquerors after the Second World War. Moreover, the U.S. government has been eager to cooperate with former Communists in Eastern and Central Europe who are op-posing nationalist factions and politicians. Leaders like longtime Communist-turned-Socialist Ivica Racan in Croatia and a former member of the Communist Central Committee, Peter Medgyssey, in Hungary, both of whom the American state department helped install as prime ministers, were seen as committed to a globalist perspective, dovetailing with American economic interests and American "human rights."[30] Furthermore, American govern-ments have insisted that former Soviet bloc countries seeking to enter NATO must undergo an American-authorized education on the Holocaust and "extremism." Such reeducation, which the Estonians refused for themselves in 2002, noting that, except for a handful of Nazi collaborators, their people had never persecuted their Jewish population (of about five thousand), resembles what the U.S. military governor had imposed on postwar Germany.[31] All of Western Europe's left-of-center parties are now advocating this form of value-education for what they see as their insuf-ficiently penitent populations.

The Post-Marxist Americanization of the European Left has been a response to the continuing need for a historically relevant Marxism. Pivotal for this American turn, as scholars on the left and right have both recognized, is Habermas's *Zur Rekonstruktion des historischen Materialismus* (1976). Such otherwise divergent interpreters as Von Beyme, Anthony Giddings, and Rolf Kosiek

---

30. Brian Mitchell, "Why Ex-Communists Hold Power in Eastern Europe," *Investor's Business Daily*, June 25, 2002, A-16; John Laughland, "NATO's Left Turn," *American Conservative*, December 13, 2002, 18–19.

31. See the remarks on Holocaust education in Estonia by U.S. ambassador Joseph M. De Thomas placed on the embassy website (May 26, 2002), www.usemb.eelholocaust;eng.php3.

have all observed that Habermas's work allows Marx's devotees to move into a new era without entirely scorning the father of revolutionary socialism.[32]

Although Marx criticized in a convincing manner, according to Habermas, the "forms of domination" that had characterized bourgeois modernity, he did not foresee fully the happy outcome of his theories and movement. Educational and scientific elites, led by social planners, would take power in the wake of the democratic-leftist ferment to which Marxism had contributed. At the time of these assertions, Habermas still leaned heavily toward East German Communism, as an approximation of his third stage of history. He reasoned that the Germans, having had a particularly evil past, needed to be pushed hard into accepting an internationalist future. By the fall of the Berlin Wall, however, an event he loudly bewailed, Habermas had turned to the United States *faute de mieux*. Here was an imperial power that, despite the capitalist blemishes that marred its social fabric, might guide Europe into a progressive global administration.

Australian legal scholar Andrew Fraser has located in these reflections those hopes that have shaped the Post-Marxist worldview.[33] The cure for reactionary values, we are made to believe, is a government of social engineers who will take a stand against what Habermas calls "the psychological residues of the past." While the Post-Marxist Left still has CP rituals—for example, denying the crimes of Stalin and Mao, declaring war to the knife against fascists, and protesting American corporate interests—at least some of these rituals have become perfunctory. In Anglophone societies these same rituals are also found in varying degrees on the left. Thus one encounters in the American press a favorable reception to the autobiography *The Age of Extremes,* by aged British Communist Eric Hobsbawm, and the *New York Times*'s fussing over

32. Rolf Kosiek, "Ein Verführer der Jugend wird geehrt," *Deutschland in Geschichte und Gegenwart* 49, no. 3 (September 2001), 17–19; Beyme, "Vom Neomarxismus zum Post-Marxismus," 125; Anthony Giddens, *A Contemporary Critique of Historical Materialism,* vol. 1, 2d ed. (Stanford: Stanford University Press, 1995), 225–34.

33. Andrew Fraser, "A Marx for the Managerial Revolution: Habermas on Law and Democracy," *Journal of Law and Society* 28, no. 3 (September 2001), 361–83.

the book of fulsome tributes to the American Communist Party by a former Communist, Vivian Gornick.[34] All of this praise underlines the continued value of leftist credentials, but describing it as Marxist assigns to it an excessive theoretical importance. Literary testimonials to onetime Communist solidarity, or the demonstrations organized for the Rosenbergs, on the anniversary of their execution as Soviet spies, are about nostalgia and social conformity rather than Marx's ideas.

Chapter 5 will deal with the Post-Marxist Left as a form of *incomplete* political religion. Like Communist and fascist ideologies and practices, Post-Marxism reveals the characteristics of a post-Christian religion of politics. It emphasizes the radical polarization between the multicultural Good and the xenophobic Evil and is willing to apply force to suppress those considered wicked. Like older political religions, Post-Marxism also claims to be pointing the way toward a future in which the remnants of the adversary (still vestigially bourgeois) society are swept aside.[35] Like fascism and Communism, Post-Marxism views bourgeois institutions, especially in this case the nuclear family and defined gender roles, as the concentrated evil that it is required to obliterate.

The current Left also engages in a transposition of Christian themes, which it weaves into a post-Christian political tapestry. It carries out a "sacralization of the political," like interwar totalitarian movements, in the only way that such a move is possible, by appropriating and disguising Christian images and myths. Such a process should not astonish us. After thousands of years of Christian education and Christian culture, post-Christian political religions necessarily take their imagistic and narrative materials from the minds and practices of those it intends to influence. In Europe the invocation of a widely diffused Holocaust blame that is made

34. For a biting description of superannuated Communist solidarity, see Sévillia, *Le terrorisme*, 205–6; see also Vivian Gornick's *A Fierce Attachment: A Memoir* (New York: Simon and Schuster, 1987). Like Bella Abzug, Gornick combines nostalgia for old party ties with a new "fierce attachment" to feminism, on which she began writing in the 1970s.

35. For studies of political religion in the interwar period, see Emilio Gentile, *La religione della politica: Fra democrazie e totalitarismi* (Rome-Bari: Laterza, 2001); Stanley G. Payne, *A History of Fascism, 1914–1945* (Madison: University of Wisconsin, 1996); and the journal *Political Religions and Totalitarian Movements*, ed. Robert Mallett and Emilio Gentile, published by Frank Cass.

to weigh on Christian societies can build on the once established Christian belief in original sin. In France Christian plaques and statues commemorating saints or the stations of the cross have been partly replaced by a post-Christian (and postrepublican) sign of suffering (and national shame), *plaques commémoratives,* particularly in Paris, and in those places where Nazi victims were arrested or from whence they were deported.[36] In the United States the same transposition has also occurred—under state auspices. While Christmas in public institutions has been turned into "holiday season," with penalties inflicted on those who violate this state-ordered concession to sensitivity, a new sacral calendar unfolds in January for school students and public employees, starting with Martin Luther King's birthday and continuing through black history month and women's history month. These by now obligatory celebrations are infused with religious sentiments, including remorse over the suffering of the innocent and the victimized in past unjust societies and the martyrdom of the assassinated King, who may be the closest that a post-Protestant society can come to replicating the post-Catholic saint Che Guevara. In these celebrations the managerial state emerges as redeemer-reformer through its role in social engineering and its work as a moral instructor. Those planners and enlightened judges associated with this regime, whether mentioned or not, are the heroes in the social transformation that democratic citizens are supposed to exemplify.[37]

But what limits the application of the concept of political religion to what is being described is its self-liquidating aspect. The multicultural ideology the Post-Marxists preach, as my book on multiculturalism argues, is a deconstructing venture, which subverts its own civilizational foundations. Above all, the emphasis placed on large-scale Third World immigration, as an "enriching" experience for Westerners, makes it unlikely that those undertaking the multicultural experiment will preserve what they are building up. Factor in a subreplacement birthrate among native Europeans, which lags far behind that of those groups whom the multiculturalists are bringing into their countries for enrichment, and the

36. For an examination of the recent manipulation of French national memories, see Henri Rousso, *Vichy, un passé qui ne passe pas* (Paris: Gallimard, 1996).
37. See Paul Edward Gottfried, *Multiculturalism and the Politics of Guilt* (Columbia: University of Missouri Press, 2002), 39–117.

chances for fashioning a long-term successor for a bourgeois Christian society look even remoter. Note that the political religions that flourished in the thirties and forties placed a high value on fecundity—for self-evident reasons. One cannot create new orders unless there is an abundance of people to fill them. Finally, the managerial nature of the present cultural-political venture prevents the Post-Marxist religion from developing sustained charismatic leadership. A distinguishing characteristic of interwar political religions, it is conspicuously absent from Post-Marxism. The advocates of the current regime have been predominantly dull, inoffensive civil servants, judges, or parliamentary figures trying to reach out to feminists, immigrants, and gays. The virile and warlike leaders of the older and more fully developed political religions have no place here.

Having said this, it may nonetheless be useful to point out the overlaps between the two traditions of sacralized, transformational politics. In their antibourgeois, post-Christian, and transpositional tendencies and in their intolerance of any social space they are not allowed to fill, the old and new forms of political religion bear a resemblance to each other that is worth exploring. By looking at political religion, while recognizing its limited applicability to the present case, it may be possible to understand the Post-Marxist Left more fully.

It might be necessary here to insert a disclaimer that in a more dispassionate universe of discourse would not be needed. Nowhere in this book is there a denial that right-wing extremists can be encountered in Europe and elsewhere. Skinheads and neo-Nazis are unfortunately present in European societies and occasionally engage in acts of vandalism. Moreover, groups that could play a constructive role in calling attention to opinions not represented by parliamentary party blocs and the administrative-judicial enforcers of political correctness sometimes include unpalatable personalities. Although the German National Democrats (NDP) may be raising useful questions about the effects of Islamic immigration and the excesses of German antinationalism that the two major blocs refuse to touch, they also carry with them unsettling baggage. Speeches by NDP chairman Udo Voigt, after his party's impressive electoral performance in September 2004 in Saxony, where they garnered 10 percent of the vote, contained alarming references to Hitler as "a great statesman."

But what this volume tries to stress is that the rise to power of the Post-Marxist Left has blocked democratic protest and the possibility of political self-correction that is not perceived as politically correct. One effect, as parties of the center-right and of the left lunge toward the imposed multicultural and postnational consensus of the current political culture, is that oppositional forces have had to find outlets elsewhere. And what serve as reference points for launching a justified protest against the control of civic discourse may sometimes be parties that are morally compromised.

To the objection that I am overlooking the possibility that those whom the Post-Marxist Left calls "fascist" might answer to that description, I shall respond by pointing out that the burden of proof remains on the accuser. And that burden is certainly not met by throwing names at someone who does not conform to the latest authorized version of "antifascism." As I try to make clear in an excursus on appearing to be the most anti-German member of an eroded German national community, antifascist name-calling is coming to take bizarre forms. It provides a subterfuge by which former Nazis can divert attention from their own pasts by accusing former anti-Nazis of being insufficiently antinationalist Germans. This German case illustrates how far "antifascism" has moved from being directed against the movement it claims to be doggedly resisting. As a colleague has suggested, it might be a good idea to preface "antifascist" with the indispensable modifier "pseudo."

POSTWAR COMMUNISM

■ The Communist High-Water Mark

The year 1945 saw the end of a devastating world war that resulted in more than 30 million European deaths, ravaged cities, and food shortages lasting well into 1947. For European Communists, however, such devastation provided causes for optimism. Soviet armies had come as far west as the Elbe River, and Soviet-style regimes took over the territories occupied by the Red Army as it pursued the retreating German Wehrmacht. Poland would be forced to abandon its eastern regions to the Soviet Union but would be given the chance to move its borders westward, into what had been Prussia and Silesia, thereby establishing (or having imposed on the Poles) a Communist government flanking the Oder-Neisse. In 1945, under Soviet pressures, a redistribution of farmland took place in Hungary, Bulgaria, and Rumania, three countries that then lay in the Soviet orbit. Because of this reform, which would eventually be superseded by forced collectivization, over 2 million families, which had been previously landless, would become owners of agricultural tracts.[1]

Although peasant and other parties in all three countries favored land reform, the Communists would receive credit for it from

1. These reforms are discussed at length in Walter Laqueur's *Europe in Our Time, 1945–1992* (New York: Penguin Books, 1992).

Western sympathizers. Indeed by 1945, mass-based Communist parties were gaining strength in both Italy and France. In October 1945, in the first postwar election, the French Communist Party received 26.1 percent of the national vote; its share would not fall below 25 percent in any election to the National Assembly before 1958. In Italy the Communist Party soared from a (still clandestine) membership of 10,000 in 1944 to over 2 million by 1947, becoming for a time the largest European CP outside the Soviet bloc. (Although the Communists in France collected more votes than their Italian counterparts, their membership lists remained smaller.) Moreover, until May 1947 Communists held cabinet posts in the French and Italian governments. The cogoverning parties were the Christian Democrats (called in France the Mouvement Populaire Républicain) and the Socialists; by 1948 these three parties were dividing among themselves over 90 percent of the electorate.[2] As the Cold War intensified, and the Communists made clear their unswerving support for the Soviet side, the anti-Soviet Christian Democrats, in Italy led by the popular, dynamic Alcide De Gasperi, broke off their cooperation with the far Left.

An obvious question concerns why the Communists achieved such electoral success in Italy and France. Their electioneering presence was minimal in the Low Countries, Scandinavia, and England, and in the first election for the German Bundestag in 1949, Communist candidates picked up no more than 5 percent of the votes. An often-heard argument is that nonrevolutionary socialist parties (like the English Labourites) carried the burden of reform politics in Northern, predominantly Protestant Europe that the Communists had to assume in Latin countries by default. Moreover, societies that had strong parliamentary traditions could achieve through peaceful procedures what the French, Italian, and Spanish working classes believed could only come about through a revolutionary party. Thus Frenchmen and Italians turned to politicians who endorsed Marxist revolution and praised the So-

---

2. See Kriegel, *French Communists,* 359–62, 378–79; and Marc Lazar, *Maisons rouges: Les partis communistes français et italien de la libération à nos jours* (Paris: Aubier, 1992).

viet dictatorship to obtain changes that could be achieved elsewhere through simple party rotation.[3]

Although not entirely wrong, this Cold War liberal explanation,
popularized by Gabriel Almond and S. M. Lipset, overlooks certain parallels between the Communist and non-Communist Lefts
in postwar Europe. The Italian, French, and English postwar governments, all of which tilted strongly leftward, carried out similar
nationalizing plans and educational programs. Furthermore, what
caused the French Communists to leave the ruling coalition in
1947 was an unwillingness to accept a cap on French wages favored by the Popular Republican Movement, a disagreement that
had nothing to do with Communist revolution. During their ten-
ure in the government, the Communists took pains not to criticize French colonialism, and they even devised justifications for
its near-term continuation; at the same time, they encouraged the
wholesale punishment of (non-Communist) wartime collaborators,
whose real offense in many cases had been nothing more than to be
known anti-Communists. Once outside the government, the Communist bosses felt free to raise Cain, organizing anticolonial demonstrations and throwing France by the end of 1947 into a series
of insurrectionary strikes.[4]

In the postwar situation many socialists, as well as Communists,
expressed pro-Soviet sentiments, and the Italian Socialist Party
leader Pietro Nenni, though not a Communist, worked to keep
the Communists in the Italian government. In a nationwide poll
conducted in France in September 1944, over 61 percent of the
respondents considered the Soviet Union the country most responsible for liberating their country; only 29 percent, by contrast, attributed this achievement to the Americans, who had borne the
brunt of the Normandy Invasion.[5]

3. Although S. M. Lipset correlates labor class radicalism with other factors,
particularly rapid industrialization, he also stresses the operation of a "relatively
moderate and conservative" trade unionism as a bulwark against radical socialism; see Lipset's *Political Man: The Social Bases of Politics*, expanded ed. (Bal-
timore: Johns Hopkins, 1981), 45–47, 73–75. See also Gabriel Almond, *The
Appeals of Communism* (Princeton: Princeton University Press, 1954).

4. See Jean Ranger, "L'évolution du vote communiste en France depuis
1945," in *Le communisme en France* (Paris: Armand Colin, 1969), 211–54.

5. Quoted in Sévillia, *Le terrorisme*, 15.

In postwar Europe the Communists exploited trends they did not initiate. Electorates swung to the left sharply, partly in reaction to the Nazis who were depicted as the far Right, and partly because the Left was considered suitable for enacting reforms that many Europeans wanted. The havoc wrought by the war increased this urgency for rebuilding societies in a way that would remove or at least lessen poverty through structural changes and income redistribution. The Soviets were widely perceived at war's end as being generally on the side of the angels, having tried to deal with some of the same material problems as those confronting Western Europeans, in a "scientific" fashion, and having lost over 20 million of their countrymen fighting "German fascism." Such views, far from being a monopoly of left radicals, were heard among "democratic socialists" such as Pietro Nenni and Aneurin Bevin, who moved slowly to rally to the American side in the Cold War.[6]

Reproducing this postwar perspective is not to defend it. Essential for this indulgent view of the Communists and of their Soviet masters was the dismissal of what in 1945 was gruesome recent history. The pro-Soviet respondents were conveniently forgetting about how the Communists in France and Italy had served the Nazis, while Hitler and Stalin had been allies from the fall of 1939 to the spring of 1941, the perfidy of the later "antifascist" French Communist Party head Maurice Thorez who, as a French military deserter, had offered his help to Hitler's army after the fall of France (on June 26, 1940), and the millions of murders committed by the Soviet state against "class enemies."[7] It is doubtful that pro-Soviet Europeans did not know at least as much about Soviet gulags in 1945 as they did about Nazi concentration camps, although the French leftist press, including Le Monde, condemned any reference to this fact (then as now) as indicative of an unwillingness to fight fascist threats. If former Italian Communist Lucio Colletti is correct that "there was a lie [bugia] called the Soviet

6. Muriel Grindrod, The Rebuilding of Italy: Politics and Economics, 1945–1955 (Westport, Conn.: Greenwood Press, 1955).
7. Sévillia, Le terrorisme, 51; Stéphane Courtois, Du passé faisons table rase: Histoire et mémoire du communisme en Europe (Paris: Robert Laffont, 2002), dwells on such Communist embarrassments as the party's and Thorez's contributions to the fall of France in 1940.

Union," lots of his countrymen, aside from CP members, had swallowed it.[8] Why they did so is another question but one that should be posed after conceding that Communists and non-Communists in Western Europe held overlapping expectations about Soviet power and that the tendency to ignore the Soviet and Communist record of oppression and treachery was not confined to CP members.

Finally, where Communist parties took hold by 1946, they did so by serving a social function—as stressed by historian Andrea Ragusa. They were "working-class" parties, a majority of whose votes and at least part of whose leadership cadres (including Thorez) were of working-class origin.[9] In Italy and France the parties were intertwined with gargantuan labor unions, the Confederazione Generale del Lavoro and the Confédération Générale du Travail; and it was only thanks to American financial assistance that the explicitly non-Communist *syndicat,* the Force Ouvrière, could take off and gain mass membership in postwar France. A working-class preponderance in French Communism was still apparent as late as 1979, when 46.5 percent of the card-carrying members were (typically male) factory workers, about the same percent that then obtained in the Italian party. Most of these members had never visited the Soviet Union, but the vast majority read the Communist publication *L'Humanité,* which incessantly described the Soviet bloc as a workers' paradise in the making. In any case the Soviets were putting up a fight against the United States, which was then supposedly trying to pull the European proletariat into an anti-Communist crusade. Resisting "American imperialism" seemed necessary to secure peace and working-class benefits in France. "Experts," typified by Frédéric Joliot-Curie, a Nobel Prize–winning physicist and party "peace activist," and the international Movement for Peace were available to confirm this judgment.[10] The French and Italian party platforms did talk about "nationalizing" or "socializing" the means of production, but so too did the English Labourites and other "democratic" socialists. Until 1959 the German Socialist Party, which the Tru-

8. Quoted in *La Repubblica,* November 4, 2001, 20.
9. See Andrea Ragusa, *I comunisti e la società italiana* (Rome: Editore Lacaita, 2003).
10. Sévilia, *Le terrorisme,* 10.

man administration had backed in 1949, defined itself as a Marxist party.

The Communist party formations consisted predominantly of male workers, most of whom disliked the Catholic Church. They viewed that institution as a socially reactionary force, albeit one that did contribute peace activist Abbé Boulier of the Catholic Institute of Paris and sent out workers' priests who cooperated with CP members. In France the Communist movement was viewed— or portrayed itself—as a continuation of the French Revolution, particularly its radical Jacobin phase, though it was also, according to Kriegel's declaration of her lapsed Communist belief, "a new stage in human history just as Christianity had been before."[11] Whatever confused dreams intellectuals may have attached to the movement, however, for workers it provided ideological identity, social solidarity, and political representation. One might fault the vehicle they chose for these purposes, but it is hard to show that these were not their purposes when they joined the party.

Among Western Communist parties there were intellectuals and artistic celebrities who formed a second tier, outside the working class and party functionaries. Not all of the adherents of this second tier belonged to the party outright, but even the "fellow-travelers" could be counted on (perhaps even more so than regular CP members) to defend specific party lines—and most particularly the special relation with the Soviet Union. Raymond Aron's widely read broadside against "the opium of the intellectuals," which was published as a book under that title in 1955, was directed against the non-CP Stalinophiles as much as it was against CP members.[12] Multiple publications came out in Paris, such as *Lettres Françaises, Nouvel Observateur, Esprit, Les Temps Modernes,* and the commentary section of *Le Monde,* that featured publicists who had not formally joined the party but who never failed to defend the Soviet homeland or to condemn its detractors. Some of these authors, like Jean-Paul Sartre, Simone de Beauvoir, Louis Althusser, and Claude Merleau-Ponty, eventually became Communists, but others, like Catholic leftist Emmanuel Mounier, railed

11. Kriegel, *Ce que j'ai cru comprendre.*
12. Robert Aron, *L'opium des intellectuels* (Paris: Calmann-Lévy, 1955); Jules Monnerot, *La sociologie du communisme et l'échec d'une tentative religieuse au XX siècle* (Paris: Editions Libres, 1949).

against the "mortal sin" of anti-Communism without joining the Party.[13]

The "issues," to use a current term, that pushed these and other intellectuals into the Communist camp were only in small measure what motivated working-class Communists. For the historian of the French Revolution Albert Mathiez and for Italian "laic" philosopher Lucio Colletti, Communism offered the promise of a thoroughly secularized society, one in which the hated Catholic Church would be driven out of public view and religious superstition rooted out. For Jewish intellectuals Annie Kriegel, Walter Benjamin, Eric Hobsbawm, and others of their background, the Communists posed a political alternative to parties and platforms that were associated with gentile nationalism or Christianity. Clearly it would be hard to separate (nor would these radicals have wanted to separate) their Communist allegiances from their fear of European anti-Semitism. Another reason that some intellectuals took the fateful plunge came from German diarist Victor Klemperer, a Protestant of Jewish ancestry who survived the war in Germany after many trials, including the bombing of Dresden. Although a liberal monarchist and German patriot when his diary opens in March 1933, in November 1945 Klemperer joined the Kommunistische Partei Deutschland in East Germany. He believed that step was necessary "because only the most decisive turn to the left can pull Germany out of its present misery and prevent its recurrence."[14] The "misery" was obviously the Nazi legacy that had brought down Germany and Klemperer's fellow Jews, including Eastern European Jews, with whom he had come to identify during the period of Nazi persecution.

Equally important for Communist intellectuals was the view of the party as a link to the resistance against fascism in World War II. Although the Communist record in that struggle was at best a mixed one, by the end of the war Communists had managed to present themselves as the most consistent and bravest *résistants*. (Their claim in France that seventy thousand of their rank were shot by the Germans has never been proved.) But such a mixed

13. For a full treatment of these engagements, see Dominique Desanti, *Les Staliniens* (Paris: Fayard, 1975).

14. Victor Klemperer, *Ich will Zeugnis ablegen bis zum letzten* (Berlin: Aufbau Verlag, 1997), 2:876–77.

combat record may have been equally true for postwar glorifiers of the resistance who became Communists. Thus Sartre and Beauvoir lived out their reenacted resistance by engaging in Communist antifascist rituals, and by wielding the epithet "collabo" against their personal enemies. What they actually did during the German occupation, which was very little, mattered less than how they interpreted their resistance, and the rights it conferred.[15] Illustrating this rite of reenactment were the protests and name-calling that Sartre and other party sympathizers helped incite, when several *résistants*, who ended up in Russia, asserted that Stalin kept people in gulags that resembled Nazi concentration camps. Among the non-French witnesses who came forth to document this practice were the defected Soviet official Victor Kravchenko and former Communist Margarete Buber-Neumann, who had been thrown into a gulag and whose husband had been shot when they went as German refugees to Russia. The upholders of the Communist version of the ongoing resistance rushed to accuse those who spoke of Soviet gulags as pathological liars, agents of American capitalism, and "the rear-guard of the Nazi enemy."[16] When Kravchenko's autobiography *I Chose Freedom* appeared in French translation in 1947, keeping the book out of libraries became for French Communists and their *compagnons de route* a part of the fight against Nazism. As *Lettres Françaises* and *L'Humanité* told their readers, Kravchenko and his malicious supporters were flooding their countrymen with "a barrage of Nazi propaganda."

■ The Search for Marxist Orthodoxy

Whatever may have impelled intellectuals to take this line, it was not in all probability belief in Marxist-Leninist doctrines or in the merits of dialectical materialism. French, Italian, English, and

15. Giles Ragache and Jean-Robert Ragache, *Des écrivains et des artistes sous l'occupation, 1940–1944* (Paris: Hachette, 1988), 69–77, 253–63.

16. See, for example, André Pierre, "J'avoue que je n'aime pas la race des apostats et renégats," *Le Monde*, July 25, 1947; André Pierre, "Comment fut fabriqué Kravchenko," *Le Monde*, November 13, 1947; and André Wurmser, "Un pantin dont les grosses ficelles sont made in the USA," *Lettres Françaises*, April 15, 1948.

other Communist intellectuals were twisting or inventing facts to
fit an existential need. As Jews, Protestants (Sartre's family had
been Calvinist), anticlerical Catholics, or extreme "antifascists,"
these intellectuals ended up as Communists or fellow travelers.
Looking at those who broke from the party traumatically in *The
God That Failed*, edited by the English Labourite R. H. S. Crossman, it is clear that dispassionate reflection had little or nothing
to do with why the contributors joined or quit the party.[17] The
moral and personal concerns that led these former Communists
into the party also caused them later to turn against it in horror.
Being persuaded by and then dissuaded of the soundness of Marx's
economic and historical premises and their Leninist glosses does
not seem to have contributed much toward getting intellectuals
interested in or turned off to Communism. While European workers became sociological Communists, intellectuals might be designated as existential ones. But neither group seriously pursued a
"science of socialism," a fact that French Communist Louis
Althusser noticed with embarrassment in the sixties. His observation, made in the preface of *Pour Marx* in 1965, ends in the rhetorical question: "Outside of the utopians Saint-Simon and Fourier,
whom Marx liked to evoke [with ridicule] and outside of Proud-
hon, who was not a Marxist, and Jean Jaurès who was one mini-
mally, where are our theorists?"[18] If Althusser complained about
the "persistent absence of a theoretical culture in the history of
the French workers' movement" and about its "meager theoretical resources," he did not mean that this movement had no ideas.
Ideas existed among French Communists in abundance, about
the therapeutic use of violence, the evils of the American capitalist empire, the role of revolutionary commitment as an existential
affirmation, and the one-sided brutality of European colonialism.
Absent from these themes, however, was an understanding of
Marxism as a "science" that could be historically verified. What
Althusser in France, Colletti in Italy, and loads of Soviet-bloc
theorists set out to do was demonstrate that Marxism was scientific at least in its own terms.

17. *The God That Failed*, ed. R. H. S. Crossman (New York: Bantam Books,
1952).
18. Althusser, *Pour Marx*, 13, 14.

The occasion for this theoretical defense of Marx's "materialist consciousness" and scientific analysis of history was the popularity in the sixties of the master's *Frühschriften*, that is, his youthful tracts, often recovered as manuscripts, going back to the early 1840s. Critical to this phase of Marx's work were *The Economic and Philosophic Manuscripts* (1844), in which certain leading ideas of the 1960s, about human alienation, the interdependence of human social consciousness and individual self-development, and the dehumanizing effects of private property and capital production, received anticipatory attention. Although mostly devoted to the division of labor in the emerging national economy, as understood by Adam Smith, and to the stultifying role of landed wealth and to the obsolescent status of landowners (themes examined by David Ricardo), what made the *Manuscripts* fashionable were the comments on man being estranged from his human and individual essence in a capitalist economy.[19] Statements of this kind can be found stretching back to Marx's doctoral dissertation in 1839 through his *Theses* on worldly and otherworldly religion, as developed by the theologian Ludwig Feuerbach (1845), to the references to economic estrangement in *Capital*. All of these remarks seemed to indicate that, for the New Left of the 1960s and for "unscientific" French Marxists, one could have a Marxist tradition that was not really materialist in its view of human nature but incorporated a humanist perspective while opposing capitalist alienation.

Buttressing this reconstruction of Marx were various writings on the young Hegel, particularly one done by the Hungarian Communist (and longtime member of the Frankfurt School) Georg Lukacs. Parallels were offered between Hegel, who had commented as early as 1802 on the dehumanizing effects of the national economy, and the *Junghegelianer*, the radical disciples of the German philosopher whose circle the young Marx had frequented in the late eighteen-thirties and early eighteen-forties. Thus Marx's early

19. For a provocative confirmation of what became the New Left reading of Marx, from the free market Right, see Paul Craig Roberts, *Alienation and the Soviet Economy: The Collapse of the Socialist Era* (New York: Holmes and Meier Publishers, 1990), 1–19. See also "Ökonomisch-philosophische Manuskripte," in *Marx-Engels Studienausgabe*, ed. Iring Fetscher (Frankfurt am Main: Fischer Verlag, 1975), 2:35–129.

writings became an extension and refinement of an essentially Hegelian analysis of history and society.[20] What these writings highlighted was the spiritual alienation resulting from life in a world that did not satisfy existential needs. Economics was the tip of an iceberg that pointed to an "irrational" society, one that did not correspond to human consciousness in what should have been the highest point in man's historical condition and one that kept concealed the material, philosophical, and political prerequisites for freedom. The Hegelian dialectic, fitting together ontological, conceptual, and historical developments, is seen as preserved in the early Marx, who remained essentially a Hegelian concerned with economic oppression. In fact this Hegelian aspect formed the keystone in the humanistic Marx. His most contemporary works were his earliest ones; his later economic writings merely reflect these interests and concerns that had emerged in his work by 1845—or else exaggerate "the materialist tendency," foreshadowed in the *Economic and Philosophic Manuscripts.*[21]

By the mid-1960s, all Marxists who wished to authenticate themselves accentuated the "epistemological" problem that had corrupted Marxist-Leninist studies. Thus German commentator Iring Fetscher, in an introduction to Marx's early work in 1975, brings up the conceptual incompleteness of the *Economic and Philosophic Manuscripts.* According to Fetscher, this commingling of philosophy and economics outlines some of the features of a market economy but "fails to examine the dynamic forces of change in a capitalist productive form." Fetscher further cites "leading scientists [of Marxism] in the DDR" that "scientific Marxist research, particularly in the economic field, remains stuck at the starting line" and "that there is no well developed Marxist method for studying the mechanics of modern capitalist activity."[22] Fetscher, an interpreter of Hegel, does not dwell on the idealist problem explicitly, but he suggests that his fellow Marxists have fallen into error by abandoning Marx's "scientific standard."

---

20. Georg Lukacs, *The Young Hegel,* trans. Rodney Livingston (London: Merlin Press, 1975).

21. See Paul Gottfried, "Lukacs' *The Young Hegel* Reexamined," *Marxist Perspectives* (winter 1979/1980), 144–55; and Lee Congdon, *The Young Lukacs* (Chapel Hill: University of North Carolina, 1983).

22. Fetscher, *Marx-Engels Studienausgabe,* 2:11.

Althusser, by contrast, minces few words in naming his villains, those who treat Marx as a humanistic philosopher or regard his later materialist work as a mere appendage to his sermons on "alienation." He goes after these misinterpreters by trying to prove that Marx was never a Hegelian. In his early work he had been a progressive Kantian who then broke from these youthful philosophical-ethical concerns in the mid-1840s. In this defense of "real Marxism" in opposition to "imaginary Marxism," Althusser emphasizes the "epistemological rupture" between Marx's "ideological phase," up until about 1845, and his later turn toward a materialist view of history. The second phase is subdivided into "works of maturation," which extend from a materialist reading of Hegel, drawn largely from Feuerbach, to the authorship of *Outline of the Critique of Political Economy*, a critical sketch of the contradictions of capitalism that looks toward *Capital*. Only by the late 1850s do we supposedly encounter the "mature" Marx, and his comprehensive economic interpretation of history. Althusser moves in an opposite direction from the New Left interpretation of the sixties by putting the "essential" Marx toward the end of his life and by casting his early work as either intimations of his examination of productive forms or as the remnants of his "ideological" phase. These ideological elements are traced back to Kant, who, like the young Marx, had affirmed the connection between political freedom and individual ethical awareness. Althusser cites the young Marx on Hegel's idealization of the Prussian monarchy and dwells on his brief against Prussian censorship in Marx's native Rhineland, both as exemplifying a Kantian influence. Althusser's genealogy makes sense in terms of what he sets out to do. Hegelianized Marxism had raced all the way from Central Europe to Paris's Left Bank, or so Althusser remarks with irritation in 1962. At that time he had sarcastically observed in an essay for *La Pensée* that "the concept of totality is applied indiscriminately to Hegel and Marx, whether by Gestalt psychologists or by Jean-Paul Sartre."[23]

Althusser inveighs equally against "mechanistic materialism," which he finds to be as defective as its "twin source of confusion, the idealism of conscience." He quotes Engels and Marx against

23. Althusser, *Pour Marx*, 47–83, 208.

simplistic materialist explanations that do not take into account those societies and cultures in which productive forms have established themselves. These mechanistic explanations ignore the political and cultural pressures that intensify economic contradictions. Althusser refers to this combination of revolutionary circumstances as *"surdétermination,"* a situation characterized by a "unified complexity" of causes. But within this skein of circumstances, a "dominating structure" *(structure à la dominante)* remains manifest, namely the power relations grounded in productive forms that drive on revolutionary reactions. Althusser is at pains to differentiate this consideration of ideological factors from Hegelian idealism, which he insists does not take into consideration political or cultural determinants any more than it does economic ones: "For Hegel the principle that unifies and determines the social totality is not a social 'sphere' but a principle that has no place nor form in society, for the reason that it resides in all places and forms."[24] Hegel applies an abstract concept, "Spirit," to political, religious, and historical life, of which particular societies are depicted as passing instantiations. Thus he winds up internalizing and spiritualizing what for Marx were social structures tied to ideological superstructures.

This venting of contempt on Hegel is characteristic of Franco-Italian socialists in the sixties who were vindicating "real Marxism" in the face of "humanistic" socialism. Thus Lucio Colletti (1924–2001) added to the charge that Hegelian-Marxists were really Hegelian metaphysicians the even more damning accusation that they were bringing into vogue medieval Catholic fantasies. The implications of this charge can be properly weighed by considering the deep anticlerical feeling found in Colletti and in other Italian Communists. In Colletti's case, an intense dislike for Catholic thought and for the Christian Democratic Party's mixing

24. Ibid., 208, 210, 102–4; Louis Althusser, *Marx et Lénine devant Hegel* (Paris, PCM, 1972). Constanzo Preve (1943–), a neo-Marxist interpreter of Marxian alienation, has written a critical study of Althusser's defense of "scientific materialism" as the core of Marxist thought, *Politique et philosophie dans l'oeuvre de Louis Althusser* (Paris: PUF, 1993). Preve seeks to rescue Marx "the humanist," preoccupied with the psychological and cultural effects of capitalism, from Althusser's picture of Marx as the historical materialist. The same points are likewise addressed in Preve's *Marx inattuale: Eredità e prospettiva* (Turin: Bollati Boringhieri, 2004).

of Church interests with political corruption was never far from the surface in his broadsides against "Hegelianizing" Marxists.

In his collected essays and later, as editor of the respected Marxist journal *La Sinistra*, Colletti rarely missed an opportunity to go after Lukacs and other "neoscholastic" interpreters of Marx's materialist analysis of ideology. Colletti rejected categorically the attribution of a Hegelian notion of consciousness to Marx or Marxism, and in *Il Marxismo e Hegel*, especially in the polemics on Lukacs and the Frankfurt School, he holds up to ridicule the scholastic hierarchy of mediated forms of being at the heart of Hegelian philosophy.[25] This hierarchy was the "critical essence" of Hegelian speculative thought that the Frankfurt School was sneaking into a leftist framework by dwelling on an essentially Hegelian idea of consciousness. This fixation and the steady comparisons of Hegel and Marx made it difficult to understand the simple axiom, that the true historical motor was the configuration of productive forces and the classes that resulted from this pattern of economic interaction. Note that despite Colletti's turning toward the right in the eighties and nineties and his ties before his death to the right-of-center ruling coalition in Italy, Casa della Libertà, he never reconciled himself to the Catholic sides of Italian life. Until the end of his life he declared himself for the Renaissance and for the nineteenth-century liberal patriots who had unified Italy. In these examples he found representatives of a Latin perspective that had not been polluted by clericalism, the Left, or the "homegrown crime" *(crimine nostrano)* of Mussolini's dictatorship.[26]

■ A Nonmaterialized Revolution

Beyond this concern with the idealist-humanist corruption of Marxist "science," Western European Communists in the sixties had to explain why capitalist economies and regimes (actually

---

25. See Lucio Colletti, *Il Marxismo e Hegel* (Bari: Laterza, 1976), 1:11–13, 13–32, 109–22, 2:357–402; and Paul Gottfried, "Marx contra Hegel: The World of Lucio Colletti," *Marxist Perspectives* (fall 1978), 138–47.

26. Quoted in *La Repubblica*, November 4, 2001, 20; see also the similar tribute on the same day by Gian Antonio Stella, "Ricordo di LC," on the editorial page of *Corriere della Sera*.

European welfare states) were not collapsing or succumbing to "internal contradictions." Why were working classes not sufficiently outraged by the earning disparities between themselves and the captains of industry to seek to change that arrangement by force? And why was there no widespread perception among the Western European majority population that their material conditions were deteriorating and would grow even worse in the absence of a socialist revolution?

The reasons for this deficiency in revolutionary consciousness become crystal clear when one looks at the French economy between 1946 and the mid-1970s. Each successive year, until the oil crisis of 1973, the French gross national product expanded by at least 5 percent, and by 1980 the income curve, which seventy years earlier had indicated wage differences on a scale of fifty to one, had shrunk, with few exceptions, to less than five to one. Although the percentage of factory workers in France remained stable, hovering around 30 percent between 1946 and the mid-nineties, other occupational changes, which did not fit the expectations of CP leadership, were taking place. Over 40 percent of the French workforce eventually became public employees, and the percentage of artisans and businesspeople shrank by half in the same time period.[27] Moreover, by the nineties the class of industrial laborers also began to dwindle, as French "employees" gravitated toward a by then expanding service economy. The agricultural sector, which Marx had properly seen in the mid-nineteenth century as a conservative force, became less and less relevant socially, plummeting in the second half of the twentieth century from 35 percent to less than 7 percent of the national workforce.[28]

A comparable economic recovery leading to social change occurred after 1945 in other Western and Central European countries, although in some places, like West Germany, it began late

27. See Jean Fourastié, *Les trente glorieuses* (Paris: Fayard, 1988); Henri Mendras, *La seconde révolution française 1965–1984* (Paris: Gallimard, 1988); and Yves-Marie Laulan, *Pour la survie du monde occidental* (Paris: Le Cherche Midi Editeur, 2001).

28. Jacques Freymond, *Western Europe since the War: A Short Political History* (New York: Praeger, 1964), 152–57; *A Decade of Cooperation: Achievements and Perspectives* (Paris: Organization for European Economic Cooperation, 1958), 24–27.

or, like Italy, went on spasmodically. By the midsixties, industrial production in Italy, Germany, and Holland was three times as great as it had been in 1914. Average real wages between 1951 and 1961 more than doubled in Western Europe and in the German Federal Republic, despite the fact that retail prices went up 50 percent simultaneously. What this meant was that internal social contradictions that were supposed to bring on revolution were becoming less apparent.[29] Furthermore, it was difficult to portray European welfare states, with large public sectors and nationalized industries, as free-market models of the kind that Marxists could plausibly describe as pure capitalism. The term *neocapitalist* surfaced in the fifties and sixties to characterize the postwar European economy, which combined a rise in wages and consumer goods with social programs and partly nationalized production. In fact, in 1946 and 1947 Communists had played a role in designing some of those reforms that had been put in place. Nor did they rule out the possibility of joining new coalitions in Italy and France thereafter. In 1955 it was not the Communists but French Socialist premier Guy Mollet who insisted on keeping the Communists out of his left-of-center government. The justified concern at that time was that Western European Communists were subservient to Soviet control.[30]

■ **The Imperialist Foe**

By the midsixties Marxists were working on new explanations for how Marx would have conceptualized later social developments; eventually left behind in this process would be the polemics that had been leveled against Hegelian metaphysics and ethical humanism. The new focus was the intellectual and political war against imperialism, a theme that dovetailed with opposition to European participation on the American side in the Cold War. This presentation of an anti-American crusade filled a theoretical as well as a visceral need: it explained why capitalism continued to flourish

29. Robert O. Paxton, *Europe in the Twentieth Century* (New York: Harcourt, Brace, Jovanovich, 1975), 545–49; Rolf Steininger, *Deutsche Geschichte*, vol. 2 (Frankfurt: Fischer Taschenbuch Verlag, 2002).
30. Paxton, *Europe in the Twentieth Century*, 548–49.

despite the economic slavery that it was alleged to be producing. The linkage of "late capitalism" to imperialist expansion was not a specifically postwar theme. Its early exponents were Lenin and Rudolf Hilferding, and before and during the First World War, revolutionary Marxists ascribed European conflict to the frantic competition among capitalist states for raw materials and markets.[31] A well-elaborated theory of imperialism as the terminal stage of capitalism was in any case available to postwar Communist parties. By focusing on the exploitation of Third World populations, it allowed Communist theorists and politicians to account for the lack of favorable circumstances for a socialist upheaval in their countries. It also helped divert moral concern about brutal suppression in Communist countries by casting a lurid light on real or imagined colonial evils.

The view that the United States was the center of a world capitalist empire was already present among European intellectuals at the end of the Second World War. Note the extended observation (October 26, 1948) of Catholic leftist Emmanuel Mounier to an American correspondent, Constance Hyslop, who had been complaining about his anti-American journalism:

> First of all my anger is directed not against the American people but only against American capitalists and American imperialists. We [French] have a strong sense of being colonized by you, like Negroes, and the way Bulgars are by the Russians. We hardly resist because in the present circumstances we know that we can do nothing without you: your credits, your machines—this is our elementary human reflex. We are poor, sick with all the diseases of war, disagreeable, and groaning like the poor, full of defects, but we are nonetheless a country of men—and not a market, certain or doubtful, profitable or unprofitable. Your innumerable "digests" that flood us seem to be a fact of barbarism, compressed, boiled down, and predigested—or so it would seem to old nations that are used to meditating and to inventing in pain—and, moreover, a mechanism of massive propaganda that bring to mind other problems. The Russians, yes, the Russians. But

31. See Rudolf Hilferding, *Finance Capital: A Study of the Latest Phase of Capitalist Development*, with supplementary comments by Tom Bottomore and Warren Lamb (reprint, London: Routledge, 1985).

the Russians are far away and we, as you must see, have tons of American paper, American ideas, and American propaganda in our bookstores. Meanwhile the presidents of our council have to follow the instructions of the American embassy before making serious decisions, and an American shadow extends across us just as a Russian one extends over the other part of Europe. And if it used to be the shadow of Roosevelt, it is now the form of a bomb and a bank.[32]

One is drawn back to these grievances in order to understand other anxieties of the time that Mounier was bringing to light in 1948, for example, the need for a workers' movement that does not reject Marxism but "surpasses it" by incorporating religious insights (whence the germ of Catholic-Marxist dialogues) or the search for a French Communist government that does not ignore the unpleasant aspects of Stalinism.[33] Mounier's major preoccupation, shared by much of the continental European Left (and significantly by the traditional Right) was keeping American influence and culture out of Europe. At the root of this anti-Americanism was a cultural-esthetic revulsion that came to assume moral and eventually Marxist-systematic dimensions in the postwar period.

Looking at this critique of imperialism as advanced capitalism sporting an American label, it is possible to trace the successive phases in its evolution. First of all, the evolving critique came to abandon a Eurocentric perspective and to take the side of the Third World, as the preferred victim of American capitalist exploitation. While this perspective can be explained by the fascination of Marxists in the sixties and seventies with non-Western socialist revolutions, in Cuba, China, and Africa, two other factors may have shaped this preference. Western Europe was too prosperous to be treated as the material basket case that Mounier describes in 1948; both its improved median wages and widely distributed consumer goods pointed toward non-Marxist economic conclusions. At the Twentieth Party Congress in Moscow in February 1956, moreover, Premier Nikita Khrushchev had exposed at least some of the crimes of Stalin caused by the late dic-

32. Emmanuel Mounier, *Oeuvres* (Paris: Editions du Seuil, 1951), 4:813.
33. Ibid., 828; and Emmanuel Mounier, "Communistes chrétiens," *Esprit* 135 (July 1947): 139–46.

tator's "cult of personality." *Le Monde* and other European publications of the Left dutifully carried this exposé, and while those who professed to be Marxists continued to take the Soviet side in international affairs, the glow was now off the Soviet experiment, thanks partly to the revelations of Stalin's successors.[34] Then, following the victory of Fidel Castro in Cuba in 1959, new centers for socialist adventures began to open up. The Parisian publishing house Maspéro specialized in books exalting non-Western Marxist uprisings and regimes; and two of its journals, *Partisans* and *Tricontinental,* abounded in praise for Castro, Mao, and Che Guevara. Sartre and his journal *Les Temps Modernes* showcased the supposed economic wonders of Cuban socialism and congratulated Castro for breaking with American capitalist-imperialists.[35]

This portrayal of the non-Western world as the center of American capitalist exploitation and redemptive social revolution has become characteristic of Marxist investigations of imperialism. An exponent of this position has been the American socialist scholar (who spent most of his career as an expatriate in France, Portugal, Canada, Africa, and the Far East) Immanuel Wallerstein (1930–). From his first published book, *Africa: The Politics of Independence* (1961) to his synthetic examinations of the present capitalist economy, Wallerstein has treated the interlocking world economic system as both politically determinative and controlled by preponderantly American interests. His contribution to comparative historical studies has been to interpret his subject from a world-economic perspective that stresses Marxist leitmotifs. Thus we are given this law of contemporary historical change: "The key factor to note that within a world capitalist economy, all states cannot 'develop' simultaneously by definition, since the system functions by virtue of having an 'unequal' core and peripheral regions. Moreover, within a world economy, the state structures function as ways for

---

34. See *Le Monde* from June 1 through June 15, 1956; and the editorial by Mounier in *Esprit* in December 1956 following the Soviet invasion of Hungary on November 4.

35. For an overview of this turning toward the Tropics in French radical circles, see Sévilia, *Le terrorisme,* 60–77. Illustrating the predilection for Castroism and Maoism are Régis Debray, *Révolution dans la révolution* (Paris: Maspéro, 1969); Jean-Paul Sartre, *Situations VIII* (Paris: Gallimard, 1971); and Pierre Jalée, *Le pillage du tiers monde* (Paris: Maspéro, 1965).

particular groups to affect and distort the functioning of the market. The stronger the state machinery, the more its ability to distort the world market in favor of the interests it represents. Core states have stronger state-machineries than peripheral states."[36]

Here one finds a restatement of the Marxist-Leninist view that the state apparatus of advanced capitalist societies seeks to exploit natural resources and cheap labor wherever possible. This practice leads to an imperialist relation that is typical of late capitalism; although the core region that benefits from economic development may continue to widen, the poor inevitably grow poorer and the possibility of revolution, born of "polarization," remains. At least some of these notions, however modified, are recognizable in *Empire* (2000), a widely sold study of American neoimperialism by the Italian Marxist (and founder of the Red Brigade) Antonio Negri and the Duke University professor of literature Michael Hardt. The Euro-American press, typified by *Time*, the *New York Times*, the *Frankfurter Allgemeine Zeitung*, the *Wall Street Journal*, *Le Monde*, *Le Nouvel Observateur*, the English *Sunday Times*, and the *Washington Post*, has beaten the drum for this "criticism of globalization" that "carries the debate over its subject to a new level of discussion."[37] (These endorsements have not prevented any of these publications from favoring economic globalization on other occasions, as an icebreaker for a new international political order.)

Negri and Hardt insist that the world-capitalist imperialism of the United States is qualitatively different from its nineteenth-century European predecessor. Unlike the old imperialists, American capitalists and politicians are not interested in direct territorial control so much as in shaping the "biolife" of those they are subjugating. Therefore they work and scheme to take over markets and culture without bothering to occupy subject peoples. The new imperialists talk in terms of global ideals inasmuch as capitalism has moved irreversibly beyond the framework of nation-states.

36. Immanuel Wallerstein, "World Inequality," in *The Present State of the Debate on World Inequality*, ed. Immanuel Wallerstein (Montreal: Black Rose Book, 1975), 23.

37. See the online reviews for *Empire* under ephost@epnet.com, especially Daniel Bensaid's comments in *Le Monde*, March 22, 2001; and Emily Eakin's "What Is the Next Idea?" in the *New York Times*, July 7, 2001.

Indeed "empire," with the United States as its material and pro-pagandistic center, now presents itself as a humanitarian enter-prise that seeks to make the world "democratic."[38]

While Negri and Hardt, like Wallerstein, pounce on rhetorical hypocrisies, their explanations nonetheless betray a lack of criti-cal analysis. The Marxism they offer, a self-advertised critique of capitalist imperialism, places Third World failures at the doorstep of corporate capitalists. But the critics do so without sufficient proof. As the economist Peter Bauer, who closely studied African and other Third World economies, tried to demonstrate, the gov-ernmental mismanagement of materially backward societies is to a large extent self-inflicted.[39] Attributing Western economic suc-cess to African suffering is to leap to unwarranted conclusions. From *Africa: The Politics of Independence* onward, Wallerstein ascribes the uneven or regressive economic developments in West Africa to its vulnerable place in the "world capitalist economy." While we are told in passing about the fragility of national structures and the overabundance of bureaucrats, Wallerstein never gets into the political habits that beset much of the continent. Movements that call themselves "revolutionary" excite his enthusiasm, despite their incitement of nepotism, theft, and the expropriation of small wealth-generating classes. All failures by revolutionary dictator-ships trying to turn the developmental corner are made into black marks on the "world capitalist economy" or else attributed to the temporary difficulty of recapturing the "greatness of Africa."

In his earliest book on Africa, Wallerstein predicts what he would like to see rather than what was likely to occur at the time, namely, that "independent African states are moving in this direction [to-ward constitutional governments] in ways not unlike those which other states used in comparable periods of their nation-building." In Hardt and Negri, the Third World exists as a form of false con-sciousness, "constructed by the colonialism and imperialism of nation-states" but bound to be "destroyed when throughout the terrain of globalization the most wretched of the earth become the most powerful being." In the emerging world of "nomadism

38. Michael Hardt and Antonio Negri, *Empire* (Cambridge: Harvard Uni-versity Press, 2001), 67–183.

39. Peter Bauer, *The Development Frontier: Essays in Applied Economics* (Cam-bridge: Harvard University Press, 1991).

and miscegenation," empire and "its attendant mechanisms of geographical and ethnic regulation of populations" will disappear, together with the oppressive figment of the Third World. Somehow what African governments do to their people has less to do with their fate than the epistemological confusions ushered in by late capitalism. And "migrating multitudes" are not people escaping from badly run countries but actors engaged in the "ethical practice" of smashing the evil empire.[40]

With due respect to the critics of American capitalist imperialism, it has not been shown that American foreign policy is consistently ascribable to economic interest. Conceivably the U.S. government might embrace foreign policies for reasons other than material profit or the quest for economic monopolies. Failing to take this broader picture into account illustrates what Karl Popper has called the fallacy of "non-verifiability." Unless Negri can offer examples of American foreign policies that are not driven by the profit motive or by some capitalist crisis, his causal theory becomes utterly mechanical—and therefore dubious. There is also the related problem of inferring a causal relation from temporally contiguous circumstances. Thus the facts that the U.S. percentage of the world's gross national product has been declining for decades, that an unfavorable American balance of trade exists, and that the United States needs fossil fuels, which Iraq has in abundance, may not supply a sufficient or even significant contributing cause for the recent invasion of Iraq. The concern about weapons of mass destruction and about Iraq as a source of terrorist activity seem to have been widespread in the United States, and particularly in government circles, at the time that invasion was planned. Whether or not the occupation of Iraq was politically wise may be left to the judgment of others; but what should be challenged is the still undemonstrated certainty that capitalist dynamics determined the military solution.[41]

40. Immanuel Wallerstein, *Africa: The Politics of Independence: An Interpretation of Modern African History* (New York: Vintage Books, 1961), 167; Hardt and Negri, *Empire*, 361, 362, 363.

41. For essays arguing that American military policies have the effect of sapping economic growth and undermining economic liberty, see *Arms, Politics, and the Economy: Historical and Contemporary Perspectives*, ed. Robert Higgs (San Francisco: Independent Institute, 1999); and Robert Higgs's commentary "How

A recent wrinkle in the Marxist critique of American imperialism is the insistence on globalist solutions as the only acceptable ones. Thus Hardt and Negri associate "democracy" exclusively with a world society, from which nation-states will vanish as a relic of the authoritarian past. When asked by a German journalist whether democrats might choose to live in a nation-state, Hardt responded that he could not imagine real democrats making such a choice. Any government other than a world socialist regime, he said, would suffer from a "democracy deficit."[42] Note that for Wallerstein, writing in the midseventies, the "persistence of nationalism" was a problem for Marxist no less than for liberal developmentalists. One could not "explain away" on the basis of a classical Marxist model the rising power of ethnonationalism on the revolutionary Left. In Asia, Africa, and Latin America one movement seemed to travel with the other, in spite of appeals to an international working class.[43] By the end of the twentieth century, Marxist critics of American imperialism were predicting the end of national identities in a dawning multicultural future.

Whence the ambivalent relation of the European intellectual Left to the American neoconservative publicist Francis Fukuyama, who in 1989 had argued that the present age was approaching "the end of history." Claiming to be a Hegelian, who believed that the end of human political development was now coming to pass, Fukuyama hailed the collapse of the Soviet empire as evidence that Western "liberal democratic" ideas would take hold everywhere. A combination of economic trade, human rights thinking, and democratic governments, modeled on the American regime, would soon make international conflict obsolete. In this emerging world, democratic citizens would be accumulating consumer goods and enjoying the blessings of political equality. Although the French leftist critic of American imperialism Emmanuel Todd devoted an entire book, *L'illusion économique* (1998),

---

Does the War Party Get Away with It?" in the *San Francisco Chronicle*, September 14, 2003.

42. Hardt, interview in *Junge Freiheit*, September 5, 2003, 7; Alexander Stille's "Apocalypse Now," *New York Review of Books*, November 7, 2000, 47–48.

43. Wallerstein, "World Inequality," 22–23; Immanuel Wallerstein, *Africa: The Politics of Unity* (New York: Random House, 1967); and Immanuel Wallerstein, *After Liberalism* (New York: New Press, 1995), 49.

and the early section of *Après l'empire* (2002) to taking apart this
"Disney world perspective," his criticism reveals an affinity with
the objects of his attacks.[44]

Like Hardt and Negri, Todd looks forward to a world society,
albeit one in which material inequalities and the allegedly ram-
pant racism and anti-Semitism that he identifies with the United
States and the American Religious Right are gone. He is optimistic
that rising Asian and African societies, in which birth rates have
been stabilized and mass literacy is growing, will resist American
imperialists and an obtrusive American "overclass." Finally, in his
vulgarized version of Hegel, which he puts in place of Fukuyama's,
history as we know it will end with the "shrinking of the American empire," which Todd asserts has already commenced. Plagued
by social oppression, unsubdued capitalism, and military overreach, the American "oligarchy" is supposedly in retreat. Todd
begs Europeans to stand aside and tend to their social problems
while the Americans overreach in their "false war against terror-
ism," which conceals the desire to maintain a hegemony that no
longer exists. If America persists in trying to demonstrate a power
it no longer possesses, it will only end by making its powerless-
ness evident to the world."[45]

What is striking about this anti-imperialist polemic, which also
shows up in Hardt and Negri, is the socialist globalist vision without the violent polarization that Marxist anti-imperialists had predicted. The new anti-imperialists have substituted what Wallerstein aptly calls the "liberal developmental model"—as opposed
to the Marxist model based on global revolutionary conflict. While
"modernization" may be preferable to "liberal," it is this first model
of Wallerstein that Todd, Fukuyama, and Negri have picked up
and adapted. Globalization, the breakdown of national differences,
and the ideal of equality are all destined to triumph, whether or
not the American empire must self-destruct before this can hap-
pen. Whereas Fukuyama writes as an American global democrat

44. See Fukuyama, "End of History?" 4; Fukuyama, *The End of History and
the Last Man* (New York: Free Press, 1992); Emmanuel Todd, *Après l'empire: Essai sur la décomposition du système américain* (Paris: Gallimard, 2002), 19; and
Emmanuel Todd, *L'illusion économique: Essai sur la stagnation des sociétés dévelopées*
(Paris: Gallimard, 1997).

45. Todd, *Après l'empire*, 130–39, 232–33.

celebrating a "capitalist welfare state," his socialist opponents demand the disappearance of American hegemony as a precondition for their globalist, egalitarian end of history. But they also opportunely argue that historical forces in both Europe and the Third World favor their version of the end times, and that the emergence of an alternative reality depends on having the Americans and their capitalist overclass step aside.[46]

This *vue d'ensemble* of anti-imperialist interpretations emanating from the European Left point to what is actually a Marxism deficit. Contrary to what is suggested by conservative and neoconservative critics of Negri, Hardt, and Todd, such interpretive literature does not betray the operation of "apparently new ideas in old Marxist flasks."[47] It underscores the increasing dilution of European Marxist thinking under the impact of changing economic circumstances and the fateful rise of American cultural and political influence. Todd and Negri may be unthinkable without Paul Kennedy, the Yale historian, who published *The Rise and Fall of Great Powers* (1988). In this comparative study of declining empires, Kennedy gave direction to later "socialist" works on the overreach of the American capitalist empire. He and another American academic, an Asian scholar at Berkeley, Chalmers Johnson, took up the themes of recent European anti-imperialist authors, before the European Left began to dwell on them.[48] And while these American interpreters examine material causes for American overreach, like their imitators, they are not specifically Marxist in their gloom-and-doom arguments. Reaching back even further, one can point to the works on American "capitalist imperialism" by William Applemann Williams and the Wisconsin school of historians. In Williams's historical writings of the sixties and seventies on American foreign policy and the expansionist needs of late

46. In *Après l'empire,* Todd reprises Fukuyama's problematic contention, drawn from political theorist Michael Doyle, that democracies never fight each other (20). For a critical view of this judgment, see my commentary "Defining Democracy Down," in *American Conservative,* September 8, 2003, 42–44.

47. *Junge Freiheit,* September 5, 2003, 7; Wolfgang Caspart, *Marxismus: Von der Revolution zur polititischen Korrektheit* (Vienna: Eckhartschrift, 2003).

48. For a review of *Empire* that skirts this observation while unleashing a diatribe against anti-Americanism, based on anti-American Americans, see Roger Kimball, "The New Anti-Americanism," *New Criterion* 20, no. 2 (October 2001), 17–25.

capitalism one finds an exceedingly detailed study of the unfolding of an American capitalist empire.[49]

One does not have to endorse all of the conclusions or accept Williams's causal links in *The Tragedy of American Diplomacy* or *The Contours of American History* (both of which have now become popular on the American isolationist Right) to perceive their relative merit. Williams's understanding of American history goes deeper than that of those self-described European Marxists who are now attacking American imperialism. Significantly, Hardt and Negri concede that European cultural hegemony over the Western world has passed from the Old to the New World as a consequence of "the crisis of Europe." All sides in Europe have come to compete as to "who could best express a strong Americanism." "The refusal of European consciousness to recognize its decline" led to projecting its utopian hopes onto the United States and "living vicariously through an American dream." Hardt and Negri poke fun at "this idea of American Empire as the redemption of utopia as completely illusory," but their scorn is mixed with astonishment about the effects of an American cultural orbit.[50] Out of increasingly destructive nationalist wars in Europe there came the European fate of being subordinate to the United States psychologically and politically. Even those who professed to despise the American capitalist economy after World War II looked with admiration to New York for avant-garde thinking and abstract expressionist art.

Equally striking are the leftist adaptations of Fukuyama's contentions about the spread of global democracy, which go back to nineteenth-century radicals John Bright, James Mill, and Richard Cobden. Such English free traders, and not the Prussian constitutionalist Hegel, created the democratic expectations associated with free trade and the availability of consumer goods that Fuku-

---

49. The German translation of Williams's most famous work, *Die Tragödie der amerikanischen Diplomatie* (Stuttgart: Suhrkamp, 1973), was prodigiously popular among Germanophone intellectuals and journalists and raced through several printings with a respected German commercial press. See also the authoritative biography of Williams by Paul Buhle and Edward Rice-Maximin, *William Appleman Williams: The Tragedy of Empire* (London: Routledge, 1995).

50. Hardt and Negri, *Empire,* 380, 382, 383.

yama has reprised.[51] What sets apart his "end of history" is the attempt to link it to "American indispensability." Fukuyama combines free trade and modernization theory with a view of the United States as the necessary means to achieve both. Significantly, those leftist anti-imperialists who criticize Fukuyama are even less convincing when they come to recycling his vision divested of American corporate interests. Like Fukuyama, they clamor for modernization consisting of liberated women and alphabetized populations in the Third World. Like Fukuyama, they also conjure up materially comfortable individuals, who can travel unnoticed across national borders—in a pluralistic world culture held together by human rights. But they exclude from this dream the prolongation of American predominance and an identifiably capitalist economy. Unfortunately for their argument, the European Left does not prove that their kind of change is taking place in the Third World; nor do they show that rival visions are doomed to fail. *Empire* ends on a suitably happy note, by having the "multitudes" invade and occupy the incipiently multicultural West, which had heretofore exploited the Third World. This apocalyptic ending turns the nightmarish finale of Jean Raspail's *Camp of the Saints* (1973), in which beggars from the Indian subcontinent overrun Europe, into a consummation devoutly to be desired. A transfer of populations provides a plausible hypothetical context for the triumph of late modernism, without having to imagine that Islamicized countries will become either feminism-friendly or pluralist. In the new futurology their populations will function as victimized minorities in a Western world that yields to a multicultural imperative. But this migration scenario is by now old hat. It builds on Fukuyama, who is both a globalist and an antitraditionalist despite the tendency to link him with the Right because of his American boosterism. Thus the radical Left turns to an already familiar story line as it depicts an "end of history" that is still, in spite of the storytellers, inseparably American.

51. Todd, in *Après l'empire*, 18–19, understands the difficulty of reconciling Hegel with Fukuyama's assertions, but he ignores the radical democratic aspect of Fukuyama's globalism; for an approving confirmation of Fukuyama's radical agenda, see George Gilder's review of *The End of History and the Last Man* in *Washington Post Book World*, July 12, 1992, 4.

3

NEOMARXISM

■ Neomarxist Stirrings

In *The Gay Science,* Friedrich Nietzsche observes that those who resisted the introduction of the modern scientific method fell back into "fabricating reasons that the existing laws should remain in force because they couldn't bring themselves to admit that they had grown accustomed to what they had and would not want to deal with other laws." Nietzsche goes on to elaborate: "Thus people have done with every morality or religion that has come along since time out of sight: one lies about the causes and intentions for the sake of an underlying habit, if someone begins to challenge that habit and inquires about its reasons and intentions. Here lurks the great dishonesty of conservatives in every age, the tendency to accumulate lies."[1]

Apparently the evolution of the Marxist Left in Western and Central Europe since the sixties reveals the same tendency, the fabricating of makeshift realities in defense of a convenient habit of thought. But those who accumulated the falsehoods, Nietzsche's *Hinzulügner,* played less of an interpretive role in the transformations of Marxism than their critics have claimed. Neomarxists, typified by the young Jürgen Habermas at Marburg, were selective about what they presented as "Marxist," and how-

---

1. Friedrich Nietzsche, *Die fröhliche Wissenschaft* (Munich: Wilhelm Goldmann Verlag) based on 1887 Leipzig edition, 29.

ever indulgent they were of Communist leaders, such choices did not signify a readiness to embrace dialectical materialism without qualifications. The course of the Frankfurt School since its founding in interwar Germany betrays what seems an ambivalent relation to Communist power. The school's members endorsed Communist regimes or expressed preference for them over their capitalist enemies but also propounded heterodox positions that Communist governments sternly and repeatedly condemned. Such a problem caught up with Hungarian-German literary and social commentator Georg Lukacs. After his hurried flight to the Soviet Union following the ascent of Nazism, Lukacs spent years frantically apologizing for his nonmaterialist dialectic. Lukacs's problems of acceptance continued to plague him in postwar Communist Hungary, and not even his desperate endorsement of Stalinist dogma and his approval in 1956 of the Soviet suppression of the Hungarian uprising could dispel the justified concern that he was not a real Marxist but a "socialist humanist."[2]

Clearly there were those, even outside the Soviet bloc, who persisted in defending what had become hardened Marxist-Leninist doctrines. But, as the previous chapter explains, their work grew difficult. Such dogged theorists fell upon disconfirming data— and upon the strategy of CP leaders concerned with a working class constituency that had no interest in apologetic tracts. Suitability for the intellectual advisory board of the Communist Party of France or Italy was different from the task of certifying one's orthodoxy for a professorship in a Soviet-controlled state. Even those Western Communists who called for Marxist-Leninist theoretical purity, like Louis Althusser, filled their discourses with enthusiastic references to Freud, Spinoza, and Hegel. And they generally avoided detailed investigations of whether Marxist-Leninist economic predictions were being confirmed in their countries. Enlarging on colonial evils was one thing; but proving in 1965 that France or West Germany was headed toward a workers' revolution because of mass misery posed a greater, and perhaps insurmountable, challenge to credibility.

2. Paul Breines, "Marxism, Romanticism, and the Case of Georg Lukacs," *Studies in Romanticism* 16, no. 4 (1977): 473–89; Paul Breines, "Young Lukacs, Old Lukacs, and New Lukacs," *Journal of Modern History* 51, no. 3 (1979): 533–46.

Economist Paul Craig Roberts has made the point that the "socialist project" suffered a theoretical setback in the 1930s, when the Austrian economist Ludwig von Mises pointed out the imponderables of social planning. Mises explained that a market system in which prices could serve as indices of popular demand functions more efficiently than do other systems. Such an economy is optimal for satisfying aggregate needs. Mises was making an explicitly utilitarian case for capitalism; and the Polish Marxist Oskar Lange devoted his own work to refuting this exploration of market efficiency. But, according to Roberts, the onus of proof remained on the socialists, undertaking to show that a government-planned economy was more "rational" than prices reflecting supply and demand.[3] The effect of this challenge was to push Western Marxists further in the direction of Neomarxism, a form of socialist thinking that borrowed from Marx with increasing selectivity. Neomarxists called themselves qualified Marxists without accepting all of Marx's historical and economic theories but while upholding socialism against capitalism, as a moral position.

It is not being argued that Austrian economists typified by Mises were alone responsible for this development. What is being claimed is that the cumulative weight of the kind of criticism Mises and his school directed against socialist planning weakened the economic foundations of Marxist theory. Thereafter socialists would build their conceptual fabrics on Marx's notion of "alienation," extracted from his writings of the 1840s. They would highlight the real or alleged material inequalities in market or quasi-market systems, to prove that socialists held the humanistic high ground. Their "quod demonstrandum est" could therefore dispense with a strictly materialist analysis and shift its focus toward religion, morality, and aesthetics.

■ Forms of Neomarxism

Foundational for Neomarxism were certain concepts isolated and then fixed on by its exponents, especially workers' democracy,

---

3. Roberts, *Alienation and the Soviet Economy*, 98–103; Ludwig von Mises, "Die Wirtschaftsrechnung im sozialistischen Gemeinwesen," *Archiv für Sozialwissenschaft* 49 (April 1920), 86–121; Oskar Lange, ed., *Problems of Political Economy of Socialism* (New Delhi: People's Publishing House, 1962), 9–10.

capitalist irrationality, real human needs, among liberationist theologians targeting Third World revolutionaries, "the preferential option of the poor," and, among Germans, "overcoming the past." Such terms held appeal beyond a Communist voting base and were intended to instill guilt in the educated bourgeois by making them feel insufficiently sensitive toward the poor and, above all, toward alleged Nazi victims. All of these concepts operated in such a way as to neutralize anti-Communist sentiment or else to shift arguments away from the practices of actual Communist governments toward socialist ideals. It is because of these functions that some critics may miss another use that Neomarxist terms of reference performed, as attempts to fortify the revolutionary fervor of Marxism after its theoretical basis had begun to weaken.

Generally, Neomarxists would be committing something similar to a Christian heresy by bestowing undue attention (thus recalling the Greek *hairesis*, that is, a selecting out) upon a particular aspect of the Marxist-Leninist tradition, to the neglect of what had been its main tenets. Thus Habermas, in his selective adaptation of Marxism, *Erkenntnis und Interesse* (1965), takes up the cognitive problem of gaining accurate social and historical information. What makes such knowledge *(Erkenntnis)* hard to extract in a nonsocialist environment is the insidious operation of class interest. Only by socializing the productive means and teaching socialist attitudes, according to Habermas, could one shatter the wall of misinformation created by existing economic relations.[4] In *The Theory of Communicative Action* (1981), Habermas reprises this argument by going after "public opinion" in a society honeycombed with party politics and economic conglomerates. According to Habermas, this packaging undermines the very possibility for the exchange of ideas that is necessary for self-government.[5] Such an argument ends up by suggesting the need for Marxist revolutionary change on the basis of cognitive and cultural issues.

Habermas also constructs a definition of "democracy" that can only be satisfied in a socialist state. Marxist revolutionary societies, whether or not the present claimants qualified as such, were

---

4. Jürgen Habermas, *Erkenntnis und Interesse,* inaugural lecture at the University of Frankfurt, published in *Merkur* (1965), 1139–53.

5. Jürgen Habermas, *Theorie des kommunikativen Handelns* (Frankfurt am Main: Suhrkamp, 1981), especially 242–65.

necessary to reverse the evils of a nonsocialist world. The point is not whether Marxist Leninism furnishes an entirely correct system of ideas or whether Soviet leaders always spoke the truth. These issues are overshadowed by an oppressive structure of authority and the trading of an ignoble form of untruth for the possibility of eventually seeing things as they are. When Habermas discusses the preconditions for having communicating individuals arrive at "norms" by which to regulate their interactions, the "fact" of material deprivation is duly remarked. Until this "fact" can be addressed through an extensive welfare state, it would not be possible, according to Habermas, to reach the "normative" level of interpersonal relations.

Despite the complaint of Marxist-Leninist hard-liners both inside and outside the Soviet bloc, the predicating of Marxist revolutionary practice upon cognitive philosophies became an established practice on the European Left. With the ascent of Neomarxism, what Colletti had dismissed in the Frankfurt School as "gnoseology," disguised as scientific materialism, gained dominance among left-wing radicals. By now what remains of a recognizably Marxist Left, for example, the several times reconstituted East German Communist Marxistische Jugendvereinigung, plays heavily on these cognitive themes. The Jugendvereinigung appeals to an "emancipated" consciousness and to the struggle against "a diseased human self-concept," which is traced back to economic exploitation and to "fascist" institutions that have still not been fully exposed and overcome.[6]

In its least complicated form, this Neomarxist scheme can be found in Liberation Theology, which ascribes a capacity for "a radical questioning of the social order" to those located at the bottom of the social heap. Thus Octavo Gutierrez (1928–), a radical priest, praises the liberating consciousness of the "disinherited," which allows them to reject a "dominant theology" typical of bourgeois thinking. Although in this teaching revolutionary impulses are given what seems a Christian justification, Gutierrez is speaking about the collective mentality conducive to Marxist

6. Kilian Kindelberger, "Potsdam, die mjv und ich," www.linxnet.de/jungelinke/history/MJV002.htm#;TOC30145783.

takeovers in the Third World: "To reread history means to remake history. It means making history from below and therefore it will be subversive history. There is no evil in being a subversive struggling against the capitalist system; rather what is evil today is to be a 'subversive,' a support to the existing domination." Gutierrez fits together talk about spiritual rebirth and receiving the gifts of the Holy Spirit with the "practice" of Marxist politics. But his Christian references do not disguise his intent, which is to elaborate on the cognitive precondition for socialist transformations. The allegedly Christian theory of human consciousness expanding through history moves easily into Marxist-Leninism, although Gutierrez leaves the economic specifics to Marxist revolutionaries.[7]

Another example of identifying socialism with advanced human consciousness can be found in Sartre's analysis of "interest" in *Cahiers pour une morale,* notes that were compiled in 1947–1948 and later published. Although not explicitly a defense of Marx or a materialist interpretation of history, this notebook dwells on the moral and epistemological limits of bourgeois life. Thus the non-socialist state provides for elections but imposes its own "bloc of interests" disguised as a choice among parties. Bourgeois politicians celebrate "abstract rights" but are guilty of a *"faux infinitisme,"* mistaking their interests for a universal good. Moreover, the capitalist creates and sustains the "myth" that he is as bound to his workers economically as they are to him. Thus the bourgeoisie conceals the disparity in the relative positions of the worker and work-giver, a situation that can only be surmounted once the revolutionary "grasps his concrete and historic duty as an individual."[8]

Sartre sounds the call for revolutionary social change while appealing to Hegel, the philosopher of history, rather than to Marxist materialism. He describes his activism as individual voluntarism, which he contrasts to "submission to the universal and abstract." Sartre's engagement affirms revolutionary socialist practice while treating Marxism as a materialist flattening out of the

7. Peter McAfee Brown, *Gustavo Gutierrez: An Introduction to Liberation Theology* (Maryknoll, N.Y.: Orbis Books, 1990), 93, 16–17, 35–36; see also Gustavo Gutierrez, *A Theology of Liberation: History, Politics, and Salvation,* trans. Caridad Inda and John Eagleson (Maryknoll: Orbis Books, 1988).

8. Jean-Paul Sartre, *Cahiers pour une morale* (Paris: Gallimard, 1983), 66–67.

Hegelian dialectic.[9] In this sense, it looks beyond the Neomarxist paradigm to what becomes, by the seventies and despite the protests of orthodox Marxist-Leninists, "Post-Marxist."

■ The Italian Connection

Another entry point for a Neomarxist approach to Marxist-Leninism came through Italian Marxist thought and the Italian Communist Party. This Neomarxism resulted from a fateful, opportunistic rediscovery of the youthful cofounder of the party in 1921, Antonio Gramsci (1891–1937). Together with nineteenth-century Marxist-Hegelian Antonio Labriola and longtime party secretary Palmiro Togliatti (1893–1964), Gramsci loomed large in postwar Italian Marxist hagiography and had his name adorning a research institute funded by the Communist Party. In the late sixties Gramsci also achieved a posthumous career among leftist academics as a "political theorist." Marxist scholars Norberto Bobbio, Leonardo Paggi, and Giuliano Procacci all published long essays on this watershed figure as an interpreter of Machiavelli and the Italian Renaissance. They supposedly resurrected the long-neglected comments on class conflict that Gramsci had made apropos of Machiavelli's treatment of the *Prince*.[10] Out of this material they drew evidence that Gramsci had been keenly aware of social struggle as a permanent aspect of modern history. In the seventies the Communist Party also brought out with fanfare new, annotated editions of Gramsci's *Quaderni* (notebooks) and *Lettere dal Carcere* (letters from prison), works that went back to his period of house arrest under the Fascists between 1924 and 1935.

---

9. Ibid., 449–50. An unpublished manuscript, "Sartre, Materialism, and Revolution" by Frederick Ritsch, makes the points found in this book about Sartre's doubtful approach to Marxist materialism. According to Ritsch, Sartre's self-ascribed Marxism supplied a spur to individual self-actualization, after he had defined both freedom and consciousness as entirely subjective categories. Freedom "refers to a plurality of freedoms" that arise in a multiplicity of revolutionary minds.

10. See Leonardo Paggi, "Macchiavelli e Gramsci," *Studi Storici* 4 (October/December 1969); V. Masiello, "Tattica e strategia nel Principe di Machiavelli," *Rinascita*, May 30, 1969; Leonardo Paggi, *Gramsci e il moderno Principe* (Rome: Editori Riuniti, 1971); and Ragusa, *I comunisti e la società italiana*, 216–20.

These works were now pulled out and showcased as part of the discovery (or rediscovery) of a long-underappreciated thinker.[11] Anglophone Marxist-Leninist historians Eugene Genovese and Eric Hobsbawm contributed to this ferment by elaborating on their own debts to the Sicilian Marxist. Gramsci had allegedly given impetus to a fresh understanding of Marx based on hegemonic cultures that radical Anglo-American historians were now applying to their research.[12]

There were also published attempts to link the by then deceased Togliatti to his contemporary in the early Communist movement. Such undertakings were intended less to enhance the status of a dead Sicilian radical than to underscore Togliatti's "reflective" side that might have been missed by those who had belittled him as a party warhorse. Note that this rediscovery of Gramsci took place at a delicate point in Italian CP history. Party functionaries and party congresses were trying to neutralize the fallout produced by the Soviet invasion of Prague, following the breakaway of dissident socialist Czechoslovakian leaders in the spring of 1968. The perceived need to continue the party's "philosoviet" stance while expressing reservations about the invasion of an "already mature socialist society" caused the party leadership considerable grief. Indeed it led to a walkout by some prominent intellectuals, who protested that the party's condemnation *(giudizio di riprovazione)* of the Soviets had not gone far enough.[13]

What the Gramsci revival in Italy aspired to do was achieve a fusion of Gramsci's Hegelianism with Marxist notions of class conflict. Although a student of Italian Hegelian Benedetto Croce and someone who identified revolutionary change with transformations

11. Guiseppe Vacca, *Appuntamenti con Gramsci* (Rome: Carrocci, 1999), 107–49.

12. See Eugene Genovese, "On Antonio Gramsci," in *In Red and Black: Marxian Explorations in Southern and Afro-American History* (New York: Pantheon, 1972), 391–422; and Eric Hobsbawm, introduction to *The Antonio Gramsci Reader: Selected Writings 1916–1935* (New York: NYU Press, 2000).

13. See the retrospective party view of this crisis of confidence in Franco Bertone, preface to *Nuove accessioni*, ed. Franco Bertone (Rome: Editori Riuniti, 1968); and the more contemporaneous attempt to strike a balance among party interests by Luigi Longo, "Rapporto sulla Cecoslovacchia," in *Rinascita*, May 17, 1968, 15–17.

of consciousness, Gramsci was now persistently presented as an enterprising practitioner of a workers' revolutionary agenda. According to one glowing defense of his achievement in the Communist weekly *Rinascita* in 1971, because of recent research, we are "now ridding ourselves of those commonplaces associated with a continuing irksome polemic against the straw man that is Crocean-Gramscianism."[14] The author did not sweep aside Gramsci's idealist side but took some of his insights refined during his confinement in the twenties and thirties and declared them as compatible with Communist theory.

An earnest Marxist-Leninist in 1971 might have felt some queasiness about "Crocean-Gramscianism" in assessing the Italian Communist Party and its cultural and sociological baggage. Into the postwar period, that organization remained heavily dependent on a Southern Italian and largely peasant constituency, a fact that only began to change noticeably in the late fifties. While Communist intellectuals were wrangling about the extent to which the party should support the Soviets, says historian Bruno Bongiovanni, they failed to address the most critical demographic facts for the future of their movement: Between 1948 and 1962 Italy had gone from being a primarily agricultural to a heavily industrial country, whose population had shifted from the agrarian South into the "superurbanized" industrial Northwest.[15] At the same time, in its publications, the party continued to reflect the formative influence of what was derivatively Hegelian thought. Gramsci and his Marxist precursor, Antonio Labriola, both Sicilians who had pored over Hegelian philosophy, were not atypical of Italian Communist intellectuals before the 1960s. Well into the 1970s "the provincialism of the Italian Left," its nostalgia for Apulian, Calabrian, and Sicilian peasant cultures and its Hegelian phraseology, elicited lively complaints from young Marxists. When Colletti launched his attacks on Hegelians pretending to be Marxists, he may have been thinking about his country's Communist

14. Eugenio Garin, "Gramsci e il moderno Principe," in *Rinascita*, July 2, 1971, 1; Eugenio Garin, *Con Gramsci* (Rome: Editori Riuniti, 1997); Guido Liguari, "Gli scritti de E. G. su Gramsci," *International Gramsci Society Newsletter* 8 (May 1996), 56–59.

15. Bruno Bongiovanni, "Gli intelletuali, la cultura, e i miti della dopoguerra," in *Storia d'Italia*, ed. G. Sabatucci-V. Vidotto (Rome-Bari: Laterza), 5:472.

traditions of thought—rather than worrying about Georg Lukacs and Sartre from afar.[16]

But this Hegelian embarrassment was turned into a definite strength when it could be made to appear that Gramsci was applying the theory of class conflict. His defenders in the academy were energetically pulling out his notes on Machiavelli to document his weight as a Marxist commentator. His depiction of Machiavelli's new order, of resourceful self-starting leaders who took advantage of the social divisions in Renaissance cities to solidify their power base, foreshadowed the "crisis of the liberal order," which had allowed the Fascists to seize control in Italy. The Fascists had not ended this liberal crisis, any more than the mercenary captains in late fifteenth-century Italian cities had prevented social changes that were then underway. And for Gramsci, a "worker's democracy," which he believed he glimpsed on a short visit to the Soviet Union, required an alteration in the political and cultural consciousness.

In his journal entries and text fragments, there was a Hegelian strategy of Marxist revolution that could be summed up as "a march through the institutions." Although not by itself sufficient for a workers' revolution, the "triumph of an advanced culture over a reactionary culture" would contribute to the overthrow of liberal capitalist institutions. Equally important, Gramsci's identification with the "Italian South" and with its "sharecropper population" *(mezzadria)* turned him into an appropriate Western representative to the Third World. Among Western Marxists it was he who allegedly best understood a model of revolution that started from the premise of a backward agrarian region. The study of a "retrograde economy" *(economia arretrata)* that the Italian Communists, including Gramsci, had been preoccupied with put them in the vanguard of a new revolutionary ideology being generated outside the West.[17]

British philosopher Roger Scruton has commented archly that the only way Marxists have made their system work is by disguising

16. See the young Colletti's call for an "animated scientific investigation of Marx," as opposed to the "scholastic fantasies" mistaken for such an activity, in "L'uomo e la scimmia," *Il Contemporaneo* 19 (May 12, 1956): 19.

17. This point was already in Togliatti's essay "Gramsci e il leninismo," in *Studi gramsciani* (Rome: Editori Riuniti, 1958), 419–44.

Gramsci's theory of class hegemony as a Marxist idea. By depicting the dominant class as molding popular consciousness, an approach that Genovese famously applied to his examination of antebellum American slave societies, Gramsci was doing something profoundly conservative, affirming the primacy of thought over the material and organizational conditions of production.[18] Small wonder that his concept of cultural hegemony has gained as much support on the European New Right as it has on the European Left. An abundance of monographs underline the role of Gramscian theories of class domination in contemporary rightist critiques of liberal democracy in practice. Scruton concludes that one does not have to be a Marxist to accept those interpretive perspectives that Gramsci believed he had extracted from Marxist assumptions. Antiegalitarianism and German idealist philosophy are its constant themes, and no matter how strategically useful he was to the Left, it was not Marxism properly understood that Gramsci transmitted to a younger generation.

Although these observations apply to what is not specifically Marxist in his thinking, Gramsci's work does relate to the Italian situation out of which it arose. For Italian Communists, his idealist points of reference and his equation of Marxist-Leninism with a revolutionary strategy were not foreign concepts but informed party identity. It was the Young Turks who had to be sold on the Gramsci revival now interpreted as a new direction. Thus when PCI functionary Giorgio Napolitano (1925–), speaking at the Fourteenth Party Congress in December 1974, proclaimed the need to recruit intellectuals, a subject on which he was then publishing a book with the party press, he was merely brushing off established Gramscian themes and making them sound novel.[19] Were not his flattering references to this *maître à penser* coming in the wake of a Gramsci revival? But what Napolitano actually said was much less interesting than what he wished his auditors to believe. If there was still a workers' cause in Italy, his speech explained, then the party had to provide well-earmarked scholarships, study groups for the young, and scrupulously tailored cultural

18. Roger Scruton, *Thinkers of the New Left* (London: Longman Publishing Group, 1986).

19. Giorgio Napolitano, *Gli intelletuali comunisti nella battaglia delle idée* (Rome: Editori Riuniti, 1975), especially 11–14.

activities. Napolitano, a Southern Italian who specialized in the economy of the Italian rural South, appealed to Gramsci while making his plea for outreach. But the same homage might have surfaced amid similar suggestions twenty years earlier. Then the old Gramsci, who was still waiting to be rediscovered, would have come up in discussions of party strategy.

A final point should be made about the PCI's march toward Neomarxism. Despite its winning performance as a bargaining agent for rural and industrial workers, the party had a problem of intellectual credibility, which worsened with the years. In 1962 at the party's annual congress, Togliatti addressed the assembled members on the glaring disparity in economic development between the "liberal capitalist" West and the Soviet bloc.[20] This contrast, which was meant to highlight the superior performance of a socialist command economy, came during a period of Italian postwar recovery, between 1948 and 1962, when the annual growth rate fluctuated between 6.7 and 7.5 percent.[21] In the postwar years, the party, moreover, expended considerable money and energy opposing the Istituto Nazionale per la Storia del Movimento di Liberazione in Italia, a study and public relations agency that had ties to the already dissolved Partitio d'Azione. This institute stressed the role of the leftist but non-Communist Azionisti in the resistance to Fascist rule.[22] Since the Communists wished to make the public believe that they had been the most effective resistance force to Mussolini, something they did not become until late in the war, they created their own publications about their role in the resistance. The pursuit of this activity was defended as an attempt to restore historiographical dignity to "the workers'

20. See "Togliatti al X Congresso," in *L'Unità*, December 3, 1962; in all fairness, it must be admitted that Togliatti was making this counterintuitive comparison about economic developments in the context of defending economic rather than military competition between the two rival blocs. He was in fact interpreting "peaceful coexistence" as a step on the road toward world socialism.

21. For detailed figures on this transformation, see Guido Crainz, *Storia del miracolo italiano: Cultura, identità, trasformazioni fra anni cinquanta e sessanta* (Rome: Donzelli, 1996), especially the figures in the appendix.

22. For what may be an overly sympathetic view of this controversy, written from a pro-PCI perspective, see Ragusa, *I comunisti e la società italiana*, 48–54. Much of this controversy is centered on Togliatti as a *resistenziale*, although the party chief spent the war years in Moscow and returned to Italy in the post-Fascist provisional government as a minister without portfolio.

movement," although there was nothing "antiworker" about the Azionisti, who were mostly garden-variety socialists.

In the late fifties and early sixties the PCI discovered a new hobby-horse, as its weekly, *Rinascita*, and the party press began publishing works by and about Third World revolutionaries. The Communist press in this period showered unstinting attention on African revolutionaries, who were presented as rebels against colonial rule or as the embodiments of a Third World literary sensibility— obviously lost in translation. Although in the sixties the French Left burned with the same passion for Third World revolution, what distinguished the Italian situation was the party's continuing preoccupation with this cultural-political initiative.[23] And one could find nothing culturally or historically specific that might explain this interest, such as an Italian empire for the Italian Left to oppose or any sizable Italian-speaking Third World intelligentsia whose work Italian Communists could celebrate. In short, the unveiling of Gramscian Marxism exemplified the PCI's frenzied attempt to be on the cusp of changing intellectual trends. And it was not an isolated illustration of the party's reaching out for respect.

■ **The Frankfurt School**

A more systematically elaborated form of Neomarxism grew out of the Frankfurt School. Its self-assigned task was to fashion a Marxist theory of consciousness combining depth psychology with a "radical" critique of rationality. The architects of this theory, Max Horkheimer, Theodor Adorno, and Herbert Marcuse, saw capitalist organization as the source of a growing anguish. No matter how the subject seeks to be liberated from the existing social and cultural situation, a scarred consciousness, which is the product of capitalist reasoning, remains. This has occurred because the capitalist productive form "instrumentalizes" reason and culture, by submitting both to a profit-driven society. With intellec-

23. See, for example, the series "Crepuscolo del colonialismo," in *Rinascita* nos. 11 and 12 (November and December 1958); and the studies produced by Editori Riuniti, starting in 1958, concerning *il risveglio africano* (the African awakening).

tual and esthetic resources being harnessed to an inhuman situation, went the Frankfurt School's lament, the only possible result is profound and deepening alienation. Because of philosophy's and sociology's turning toward "scientism," Horkheimer explains, it is necessary to find a "theory of society" that is dramatically different from the one adopted by the young Marx. In his investigation of the political economy, Marx had uncovered the material sources of the social dialectic. But, as Horkheimer stresses in his remarks at his inauguration as new director of the institute, "the present situation" demands a historically specific approach to the crisis of bourgeois society. The "narrowing of rationality" (Verengung der Rationalität) is supposedly precluding the possibility for effective social criticism. And one should not try to circumvent this challenge by coming up with "mere positivist descriptions" of what is going on in the social sphere.[24] Adorno expressed the same concern by waging a lifelong vituperative battle against "administrative sociology," as an avoidance of coming to terms with the contradiction between the satisfaction of human psychic needs and rigid social structures.[25]

In *The Dialectic of the Enlightenment*, which Adorno and Horkheimer prepared during the early forties in Los Angeles, we learn about the fateful link between "the domination of and the capitulation to Nature" (Naturbeherrschung und Naturverfallenheit). Looking back at the figure of Odysseus as depicted by Homer, Adorno and Horkheimer find there the "primitive image of the bourgeois individual" who is made to sacrifice himself for the sake of human advancement. Unlike the socialist vision of a society in which human sacrifice and renunciation will no longer be necessary, the bourgeois builds a world of deferred expectation. He thus comes to resemble Odysseus, who had to be chained to the mast of his ship lest he and his sailors succumb to the Siren's song and crash against the shoals: "The bargaining away of the sacrificial victim for the sake of self-preserving rationality involves

24. Max Horkheimer, "Die gegenwärtige Lage der Sozialphilosophie und die Aufgabe eines Instituts für Sozialforschung," in *Frankfurter Universitätsreden* (Frankfurt am Main, 1931) 37.
25. This criticism about the institutional use of the social sciences is in Theodor Adorno's *Stichworte: Kritische Modelle 2* (Frankfurt am Main: Suhrkamp, 1969).

an exchange no less than a sacrifice. The persisting self that emerges from this ordeal of sacrifice is itself a hard, stony sacrificial ritual that man, since he must oppose his own consciousness to the natural world, continues to celebrate."[26]

Adorno in particular was absorbed in a "civilizational critique" that made the point that the price of wresting material power from Nature was the sacrifice of both intellectual independence and "true subjectivity." This concern pervades his address "Late Capitalism or Industrial Society?" given at the German Sociologists' Conference in Frankfurt in 1968. "It might be considered whether the present society can give birth to a coherent social theory. Marx had it easier, because his path to science lay through a fully developed liberal system. Marx only had to ask whether capitalism in its dynamic stage corresponded to its model in order to bring forth in contrast to the received theoretical system his own related counter-theory. Nonetheless the market economy has become so riddled with holes that it defies any such contrast. The irrationality of the present social structure impedes the rational unfolding of the theory. The perspective that control of the economic process has gone to those in political power comes from the dynamics of the system and tends toward objective irrationality. That, and not merely the sterile dogmatism of its followers, helps to explain why we have not yet produced a convincing objective social theory."[27]

While Adorno and other members of the Frankfurt School continued to speak of "reason" and "objectivity," what they saw as the controlled "irrationality" of the existing "late capitalist" society made it difficult to investigate that society in a comprehensive, systematic way. The deeply engaged researchers made it clear, when they set up *Zeitschrift für Sozialforschung* in 1931 as the organ of the Institute for Social Research in Frankfurt, that the most enlightening approach for social and cultural studies was subjective theorizing. Adorno carried this so far that in 1961, while collaborating with Horkheimer in a foreword to their joint work *Sociologica II,* he submitted "a bunch of observations without a full-fledged

26. Theodor Adorno and Max Horkheimer, *Dialektik der Aufklärung: Philosophische Fragmente* (Amsterdam: Querido, 1947), 70.

27. Theodor Adorno, *Gesammelte Schriften* (Frankfurt am Main: Suhrkamp, 1972), 8:359.

theory." Given the irrational society in which they lived, it seemed irresponsible, said Adorno, to offer an "objective" analysis of what seemed unintelligible.[28] What became for him and Horkheimer and their disciples "critical theory" was an accretion in various areas of research of impressionistic judgments framed by self-aware subjects who understood the cultural problems of late capitalism.

Adorno applied this critical awareness to a multiplicity of subjects, including atonal music, reassessments of the Hegelian dialectic, depth psychology, expressionist art, and "fascist" social attitudes and behavior. Out of the spontaneity of freely developing associations of sound in modern music, Adorno found something promising that leads beyond a society in which "the attempt to dominate Nature had yielded to blind forces." Subjectively music and art, by shocking the listener or observer, calls attention to "what is unbearable in the present situation." It was offering both an "image of what does not exist" and a dialectical possibility of moving beyond what is, through an esthetic intimation of an alternative reality. The artistic or musical innovator was defying the "culture industry" that had commodified what is meant to be a true expression of subjective imagination.[29]

But not all subjectivity, as seen by the Frankfurt School, was equally worthy of respect. Lurking in those who were not properly critical or had not risen above popular prejudice was a sadomasochistic personality that Frankfurt School intellectuals worked to probe. From *Studien über Autorität und Familie,* published as a collective Frankfurt School project after the organization was transferred to the United States in 1934, to *The Authoritarian Personality,* which Adorno put together during and after the war, relying on a sympathetic team at Berkeley, and brought out with the financial backing of the American Jewish Committee, the critical theorists after the rise of Nazism took on the psychological roots of authoritarian and profascist mentalities. This may be their most enduring contribution to the social-engineering Left, for these works

28. Quoted in Rolf Wiggershaus, *Theodor W. Adorno* (Munich: C. H. Beck'sche Verlagsbuchhandlung, 1987), 99.

29. See Rolf Wiggershaus, *Die Frankfurter Schule: Geschichte, theoretische Entwicklung, politische Bedeutung,* 6th ed. (Munich: Beck'sche Verlagsbuchhandlung, 2001), 566–90; and Martin Jay, *Adorno* (Cambridge: Harvard University Press, 1990).

emphatically urge progressive state administrators to deal with "latent anti-Semitism" and other forms of "pseudo-democratic" expressiveness. A thematic line leads from the investigation done by Eric Fromm in *Studien,* concerning the reemergence of the "patriarchal household" and its accompanying repressiveness, to the indices of "fascist personalities" that are found in *The Authoritarian Personality.* Adorno feared that those measurements he applied in looking for "unprejudiced" personalities did not detect all right-wing aberrations with sufficient thoroughness.[30] Because of the anti-Communist environment of postwar America and the ultimately antirevolutionary character of democratic welfare states, even those who might have seemed progressive nonetheless carried ominous personality traits. That is to say, even those who went along with economic redistribution, held a sympathetic view of the Soviets, and deplored anti-Semitism, sexism, and racism, Adorno explained to Horkheimer, continued to exhibit characteristically fascist attitudes. Note that for Adorno and his collaborators emotional disorder was inherent in late capitalism, despite the fact that welfare states tried to address economic crises and provided for a minimal general standard of living.

How, might it be asked, are such positions to be considered "Marxist"? Already back in the forties penetrating critics poked fun at Critical Theory as a mélange of Hegelian, Freudian, and (for a while) Jewish messianic views that never really added up to Marxist-Leninism. In defense of this project as a Marxist one, it might be said that its practitioners regarded themselves as revolutionary disciples of Marx and took pains to place their work into a Marxist framework. The contributors to the *Studien* took Freud to task repeatedly for ignoring the socioeconomic factors behind neurotic behavior, and Marcuse and Horkheimer made it clear that the "family crisis" sprang from the destructive effects of late capitalism.[31] Because of the failure of a bourgeois liberal society to give way to a Marxist socialist one, certain pathologies had come to prevail within the household. Like the authoritarian state

---

30. Wiggershaus, *Die Frankfurter Schule,* 467–70.
31. *Studien über Autorität und Familie* (Paris: Institut für Sozialforschung, 1936).

that organized late capitalism and the working class in a repressive manner, the patriarchal family was achieving new life. Women were now stripped of that "limited sphere of freedom" they had once enjoyed in the home during the heyday of liberal bourgeois society.

In the recent Western past, Horkheimer reminds us, the entrepreneurial bourgeois had created a general social model that had left women in charge of domestic arrangements, and even those below the ruling class had tried to imitate their family life. Now both spouses had become subject to arbitrary male dominance and to an oppressive state, allied to an inhuman economy. They were raising children in a sadomasochistic fashion, and the absorption of this behavioral model by the younger generation further strengthened the repressive power of the state.[32] The lack of humane socialist alternatives, according to the Critical Theorists, had resulted in the family becoming a hothouse of psychic disorders.

Adorno, Marcuse, and other members of the Frankfurt School were explicit about the link between "antifascism," which was the banner they sported, and sympathy for Communist governments. Like Sartre and his collaborators at *Les Temps Modernes,* the Critical Theorists considered anti-Communist attitudes proof positive of fascist residues in those who expressed them. After the publication of *The Authoritarian Personality* in 1950, Adorno was shocked by a suggestion from one of his coworkers, Seymour Martin Lipset, that the psychic grid they had applied to right-wingers might work for left-wing extremists equally well. Such ideas drove home for Adorno the anti-Communist hysteria that he thought raged on the democratic Left.[33]

His anti-anti-Communism, which in Adorno's case meant a general indifference to Communist assaults on personal and social liberties, became a characteristic of many Frankfurt School intellectuals. What changed from the master to his best-known disciple, Habermas, according to Adorno's biographer Rolf Wiggershaus, were the moral grounds invoked for turning a blind eye to Communist tyranny. Those grounds went from the need to indulge an

---

32. "Allgemeiner Teil," in ibid.; Max Horkheimer, *Zur Kritik der instrumentellen Vernunft* (Frankfurt am Main: Suhrkamp, 1967).
33. Quoted in Lasch, *True and Only Heaven,* 451.

imperfect representation of a Marxist society to providing penance for Germans and others who had internalized the fascist past.[34] Whatever the reason for this need to defend or palliate Communist states, it is a Neomarxist trait that has little to do with Marxist economics or a Marxist historical interpretation.

Is the critical observation about the Frankfurt School therefore correct, that it exemplifies "cultural Bolshevism," which pushes Marxist-Leninist revolution under a sociological-Freudian label? To the extent its practitioners and despisers would both answer to this characterization, it may in fact be valid. But a question posed by an Austrian critic, Wolfgang Caspart, might justify reconsidering this provisional affirmative response. According to Caspart, "the cultural Bolsheviks, who seethe with resentment, have altered the climate of opinion [in Europe] and shifted the cultural center leftward but in no way have they damaged capitalism or brought about a revolutionary change in the ownership of the forces of production. Although PC Neomarxism does seem to be thriving, it has become a spongy, increasingly abstract concept whose proponents more than fifty years after the deaths of Hitler and Mussolini have nothing to talk about except 'antifascism.'"[35] Despite his presentation of wannabe Marxists, Caspart insists that he is depicting real ones, who have transposed revolutionary materialism into a radical cultural framework. What remains, once this transposition takes place, is hatred of bourgeois society, which is made synonymous with "fascism." And equally Marxist, according to Caspart, is the desire to replace European nation-states with a revolutionary internationalist society and with an expanding political control over citizens in order to "reeducate" them.

All of this may be true, but if Marxism under Frankfurt School leadership has undergone the alterations indicated by Caspart, then there may be little Marxism left in it. The appeal of the Critical Theorists to Marx has become increasingly ritualistic and what there is in the theory of Marxist sources is now intermin-

---

34. Wiggershaus, *Theodor W. Adorno*, 135–36.

35. Caspart, *Marxismus*, 69. Although by no means the only author who links the Frankfurt School to orthodox Marxist-Leninism, Caspart first asserts and then implicitly denies this connection. The invocation of "cultural Bolshevism" as a conceptual bridge between the two leftist camps does not prove the underlying premise about Marxist continuities.

gled with identifiably non-Marxist ones. From medieval Jewish mysticism in the philosopher Walter Benjamin to Horkheimer's appropriation of Schopenhauer and his philosophy of the will, to Fromm's and Marcuse's incorporation of depth psychology and Adorno's musings about the Hegelian dialectic and atonal musicology, the Frankfurt School has incorporated a salmagundi of ideas framed in notoriously murky prose. Relating these interests to a Marxist social framework while being pro-Communist or at least anti-anti-Communist may have bestowed on these authors and their sponsors a leftist cachet. The same is equally true of Sartre, who mixed his existentialist individualism and psychoanalysis with Marxist politics. But was the end product of these Neomarxist commitments a reformulation of dialectic materialism; or were European leftist intellectuals doing something rather different? In a nutshell, they had moved beyond Marxism, or were lurching back and forth between Marxism and other movements, while continuing to pay lip service to Marxist theory and Communist politics. But ultimately they evolved from what has been called Neomarxism into a militantly antibourgeois stance that operates independently of Marxist economic assumptions.

■ The Americanization of the Frankfurt School

Ties were developed in the thirties and forties between the Frankfurt School and the American academy and the American publishing industry, and this productive friendship continued to flourish into the sixties and seventies. Works on social psychology and social criticism that emanated from the Frankfurt School were published in English in the United States, presumably for American readers, who subsidized their research and paid for their books. What marked this transmission was not the reluctant or isolated absorption of what can be called foreign substances. Adorno spent only twelve years in the United States, but he returned to his favorite residence, in California (on one occasion for as long as a year), after being induced (really heavily bribed) to take a post at the University of Frankfurt in 1949. This outspoken social radical took considerable pains to hold on to his American citizenship and spent his American royalties in his adopted country. Despite his expressed concern that the United States and its allies were "impeding the progress of socialist freedom" by harassing Communist parties, which "are the only genuine anti-fascist force," Adorno and his colleagues worried about deportation.[36] The desire of his friends to stay in America distressed Horkheimer, who was emotionally attached to the Old World. In 1951, while rector at the University of Frankfurt, and hoping to reestablish the Institut für Sozialforschung in the city of its founding, Horkheimer tried desperately to lure his old circle back to Europe. Few of them would implement the career change he tried to persuade them to make.[37]

Frankfurt School stalwarts Herbert Marcuse, Otto Kirchheim, Karl Wittfogel, Eric Fromm, Wilhelm Reich, and Karen Horney built up American followings and connections and, save for the erotically obsessive Reich, succeeded in the United States professionally and financially. Horney and Fromm became recognized leaders in American psychoanalysis and by the late thirties were publishing in English almost exclusively. Even before *The Authoritarian Personality,* Horney's *The Neurotic Personality of Our Time* (1937) and *New Ways in Psychoanalysis* (1939) and Fromm's *Escape from Freedom* (1941), *Man for Himself* (1947), and *Psychoanalysis and Religion* (1950) had established a vigorous Frankfurt School presence in the United States. Nor is it correct to assume that this fame was based entirely on the popularization of psychoanalytic techniques. Horney, an early advocate of feminist issues, believed that the social structure strongly imprinted those psychic drives analyzed by Freudian psychology. Like Fromm, Horney agonized over the tyranny of the superego, the Freudian censoring mechanism, which in a patriarchal society becomes overly dominant.[38] Fromm's first book, which sold well in English translation, *Die Entwicklung des Christusdogma* (1930), took as its theme the destructive link between Christianity and the authoritarian personality. Fromm believed that both capitalism and the degeneration of

---

36. Wiggershaus, *Die Frankfurter Schule,* 434–35.

37. See the closing section of Martin Jay, *History of the Frankfurt School and the Institute for Social Research, 1932–1950* (University of California Press, 1996).

38. Wiggershaus, *Die Frankfurter Schule,* 296–314; Karen Horney, *The Neurotic Personality in Our Time* (New York: Norton, 1994); Karen Horney, *New Ways in Psychoanalysis* (New York: Norton, 1988).

Jewish belief into a Christian heresy were problems whose effects could still be seen. Both had laid the foundation for a sado-masochistic culture and for the predictable rise of fascism.[39]

The psychoanalytic side of Frankfurt School research was never a mere "therapy to be applied to individuals without reference to the general social situation." Although members of the group had differed about the degree to which they were to be connected, it was assumed by Critical Theorists that depth psychology was to go "beyond Freud" by being anchored in social consciousness. An early advocate of this linkage, Marcuse underlines it in books that ran through numerous American printings, *Eros and Civilization* (1950), *One Dimensional Man* (1961), *An Essay on Liberation* (1969), and *Counterrevolution and Revolt* (1972). His tendency to politicize erotic expressiveness, while treating capitalism as sexually repressive, goes back to his hard-line stand of the early thirties. An exponent of psychoanalysis as a revolutionary Marxist instrument, the young Marcuse held no brief for those "technical analysts" who interpret neuroses as a primarily individual problem.[40]

While overly sharp distinctions between the two should be avoided, there are certain themes that dominate the Frankfurt School's American work far more than their European. Adorno's tracts on music, the dialectic, and phenomenology seem aimed at European readers, and none of them, even in translation, has done well in the Anglophone world. It was Adorno's examination of "latent anti-Semitism" and his ventures into social psychology that sold best in the United States. The social criticism directed at prejudice fitted into the American reform environment for which the struggle against Nazi racism continued to be meaningful. Nurturing this environment was Gunnar Myrdal's fifteen-hundred-page exploration of American racial discrimination, *An American*

39. Wiggershaus, *Die Frankfurter Schule*, 164–65; and Eric Fromm, *Die Entwicklung des Christusdogma: Eine psychoanalytische Studie zur sozialpsychologischen Funktion der Religion* (Munich: C. H. Beck'sche Buchhandlungsverlag, 1965); Eric Fromm, *The Sane Society* (New York: Henry Holt, 1990); Eric Fromm, *Escape from Freedom* (New York: Henry Holt, 1994); Eric Fromm, *From the Anatomy of Human Destructiveness* (New York: Holt, Rinehart, and Winston, 1973).

40. Wiggershaus, *Die Frankfurter Schule*, 172–73; Herbert Marcuse, *One-Dimensional Man: Studies in the Ideology of Advanced Industrial Societies* (Boston: Beacon Press, 1991); Herbert Marcuse, *Counterrevolution and Revolt* (Boston: Beacon Press, 1989).

Dilemma (1944). Despite its daunting size and not always idiomatic prose, characteristics that apply to *The Authoritarian Personality* *(TAP)* equally, Myrdal's extended attack on the racial double standard received thunderous approval from American progressives.[41] It yielded a theoretical and hortatory justification for those reforms that the American government was undertaking in the postwar period.

Unlike the book done by the Swedish sociologist and friend of Adorno's, *The Authoritarian Personality* did not become a reference work for those writing judicial decisions against segregation. But for many it seemed an equally useful guide for social improvement. By the sixties and seventies, the Frankfurt School's crusade against prejudice achieved widespread American acceptance and was reflected in landmark legislation and administrative directives concerning women's rights, the punishment of antiblack behavior, the further secularization of society, and later, the obligatory tolerance of gays. In *The True and Only Heaven,* Christopher Lasch makes the provocative point that the Frankfurt School's war against prejudice was particularly suited for a state and society that accepted the value of politically imposed behavior modification. This moral zeal for social planning and the application of therapeutic techniques were becoming apparent around the same time that the Frankfurt School in exile was making its influence felt. Although "only one of many postwar studies to argue — that the people as a whole had little understanding of liberal democracy and that important questions of public policy should be decided by educated elites," Lasch considers *TAP* a precursor of later sociological studies. Public policy elitism in conjunction with "sociological determinism" drove forward the work of redefining "democracy" as an antidemocratic practice.[42] Lasch offers his criticism not as a

---

41. Gunnar Myrdal, *An American Dilemma: The Negro Problem and Modern Democracy* (New York: Harper and Row, 1962); David Southern, *Gunnar Myrdal and Black-White Relations* (Baton Rouge: Louisiana State University Press, 1987); Pat Schipman, *The Evolution of Racism* (New York: Simon and Schuster, 1994); Jared Taylor, "Sowing the Seeds of Destruction," in *A Race against Time: Racial Heresies for the Twenty-First Century* (Oakton, Va.: New Century Books, 2003).

42. See Lasch, *True and Only Heaven,* 560; Wiggershaus, *Die Frankfurter Schule,* 390–478; and Theodor W. Adorno (with Else Frenkel-Brunswick, Daniel J. Levinson, R. N. Sanford, et al.), *The Authoritarian Personality* (New York: Harper and Brothers, 1950), especially 442–84 and 676–85.

defender of the free market but as a socialist, albeit of a sui generis kind. In his view, the Left had abandoned legitimate concerns about providing family support in order to work against traditional gender roles and religious beliefs. Lasch is particularly upset that the advocates of this therapeutic radicalism had left behind the working class as a reactionary force.[43]

The True and Only Heaven may be cited to confirm that the Frankfurt School's Neomarxism had grown into a Post-Marxist cluster of attitudes and programs that traveled easily in American society. The Americanized version of Critical Theory provided resources that served well in a therapeutic war against bigotry. In this struggle, Critical Theory enjoyed the aid of federal and state agencies and the blessings of the media and entertainment industries, which protested (sometimes after the fact) what they considered to be long-lived prejudices. While such ideas had an explosive effect, they did not, as Caspart correctly concedes, bring about the kind of economic changes that might be accurately called Marxist-Leninist. And this success was not working-class driven, a fact that Adorno and Horkheimer had already observed by the 1940s when they complained that American workers favored patriarchal, authoritarian institutions.

An often forgotten phase of Adorno's life may further illuminate his relation to the United States. Soon after his return to Frankfurt in 1949, he undertook a project for the institute, "Gruppenexperimente," that received generous funding from the U.S. High Commission in Germany. In this project, which consisted of interviews with German citizens and their subsequent evaluation by Adorno and his coworkers, an attempt was made to detect "fascist sympathies" in Germans then undergoing American-led "reeducation." As Adorno's biographer Lorenz Jäger stresses, the interviewers, who in some cases had shady Nazi pasts, blurred the distinction between fascist loyalties and well-founded observations about the recent past.[44] For example, Germans who complained about the Allied bombing of the German civilian population

43. See Lasch, *True and Only Heaven*, 460–61; and S. M. Lipset's defense of the Frankfurt School on "working-class authoritarianism" in the *American Sociological Review* 24 (1959): 482–501.
44. Lorenz Jäger, *Adorno: Eine politische Biographie* (Stuttgart: DVA, 2003), 219–21.

during the war, or about the American treatment of the defeated
Germans immediately afterward, or who noted the harshness of
the Treaty of Versailles ending World War I, were presumed to be
sympathetic to Nazism or else written off as mentally troubled
German nationalists. But these anti–Frankfurt School observations
were entirely defensible, as Jäger explains, and were shared by
German Social Democratic leader Kurt Schumacher, who had
spent the war years in a Nazi concentration camp. Adorno had become the shrill voice of the American victors, who were still angry
with the Germans as their wartime enemies and shocked by the
discovery of Nazi atrocities. His "Gruppenexperimente" also became a bridge between Adorno's short-lived Teutonophobia and
his encouragement of Allied "reeducation" and the leftist career
of his soon-to-be-converted protégé Habermas.

Whether or not responsible for the final product, the Critical
Theorists who took up residence in the United States furnished
the tools and themes of the Post-Marxist Left. Their work pointed
toward a Left that could rally young professionals pursuing untradi-
tional lifestyles. In Europe a sociologically related Left demanded
a break from the bourgeois past, identified as outmoded and incipiently "fascist." (The French and Germans have invented names
for this stigmatized past that endures into the present, *ringardise*
and *Ewiggestriges*.) The Post-Marxists still extract their demoniz-
ing labels from the Communist Popular Front of the 1930s but
apply them to a cultural situation that is clearly different. And the
Frankfurt School remains relevant, partly by paving the way for
this widespread, risible practice. Frankfurt School theorists constructed a definition of "fascism" that could be extended rhetorically to anything deemed unprogressive or insensitive. This may
not have been their only conceptual achievement, but historically
it was their most significant.

4

THE POST-MARXIST LEFT

■ Communist Disintegration

By the 1980s the stage was set for the rise of the Post-Marxist Left. The large working-class constituencies that had voted for the French and Italian Communist parties and had swelled their membership lists were shrinking rapidly. The workforce throughout Western Europe was changing occupationally and sociologically as countries were moving toward service economies. While French party membership in 1979 consisted of at least 45 percent industrial and farm workers, by 1997 that figure had gone down to 31 percent. Moreover, in 1994, despite the objections of older members, the PCF ceased to refer to itself as the "party of the working class." By 1997 well over half the party members were white-collar employees and professionals.[1]

A related phenomenon that Scott Lash and John Urry discuss in their book *The End of Organized Capitalism* has been the disintegration of "organized capitalist relations" and its spatial and cultural dimensions. As production has been moved away from factory cities and become decentralized, the relations that once flowed out of a capitalist social system have dissolved. Workers in Europe no longer identify themselves as strongly as they once did

---

1. See François Platone, "Le vote communiste: Le verre à moitié plein," in Pascal Perrineau and Colette Ysmal, *Le vote surprise: Les élections legislatives du 25 mai et 1er juin 1997* (Paris: Presses de Sciences-Po, 1998), 161–88.

as a class, while their neighborhoods and distinctive ways of life are in the process of vanishing. Lash and Urry see this working-class life as supplanted by a "postmodernist sensibility," which finds expression in a pervasive pop culture.[2] These changes and a rise in the general living standard have brought about a blurring of the social lines, which go back to the nineteenth century, between the industrial and financial bourgeoisie and what used to be the proletariat. Although not equally apparent in all countries, the working-class vote has shifted rightward in both France and Italy. A growing discontent with Third World immigration, thought to aggravate violent crime and to depress wages, has pushed French and Italian workers toward parties, almost invariably on the nationalist Right, that oppose further immigration. Parties on the left have been generally powerless to counteract this, because of their attempted alliance with Third World immigrants and their crusade against "racism."[3]

The fall of the Soviet Union and of Eastern European Communist regimes by 1989 accelerated the weakening of Communist parties in Western Europe, which were tied internationally to the Soviet orbit. But it would be wrong to assign too much weight to this turning point. Communist membership in France and Italy was on the wane by the eighties, even before the Soviet implosion had taken place. Economic and demographic transformations had made the social confrontations on which Communism had thrived a thing of the past. Surveys of the PCF taken in 1997 indicate that support for the party as the vanguard of the working class and for the "accomplishments" of the by then collapsed Soviet republics in Eastern Europe was correlated to age. Those over sixty or those who had been members since before 1958 leaned heavily toward the once established views about Communists in power. Those under thirty had little interest in either position.[4]

But new social fissures had opened up by the sixties that the

2. Scott Lash and John Urry, *The End of Organized Capitalism* (Madison: University of Wisconsin Press, 1987), 285–314.

3. See Pascal Perrineau, "La dynamique du vote Le Pen: Le poids du gaucho-lepénisme," in *Le côté de crise: L'élection présidentielle de 1995* (Paris: Presses de Sciences-Po, 1995), 243–61.

4. François Platone and Jean Ranger, "Les adhérents du Parti Communiste Français en 1997," *Enquête: Les Cahiers du CEVIPOF,* 27 (March 2000).

European Left, whether Socialist or Communist, would have to accommodate. Already foreshadowed by the protest movements of the late sixties that spread across Western Europe and the United States, this wave of mostly youthful rebellion was directed explicitly at bourgeois society—or at whatever was left of it. In its most extreme form this protest against the Vietnam War, the installation of Pershing Missiles by the American military on European soil, and a "repressive" bourgeois culture produced serial violence.[5] This anti-American fury was typified by the Baader-Meinhof Gang in Germany, the Brigate Rosse in Italy, and the Weathermen in the United States, all of which groups engaged in terror and sometimes murder to express their contempt for militarism and bourgeois values. In Germany the outpouring of anger turned sharply antinationalist, as university students condemned their parents as accomplices or stooges of Nazi tyranny. Thus was visited on the parents the fruits of American postwar reeducation, in a way that would bring regret to some of the reeducators. Locked in a struggle with Soviet Communists, the Americans found Germans who claimed to be expiating the Nazi past on the wrong side of the Cold War.[6]

As this violent protest movement abated, its onetime members became politicians and journalists who, by the late twentieth century, formed a Pleiades of European celebrities. The current German foreign minister, Joschka Fischer, who in 1999 announced that "Auschwitz is the founding myth and moral justification" of a continued German nation-state, had been closely associated with left-wing terrorists in the sixties and early seventies.[7] Former French premier Bernard Jospin, French Socialist senator Henri Weber, *Le Monde* editorial director Edwy Plenel, and a leading academic philosopher, Daniel Bensaïd, are only a few of the French dignitaries who in the sixties had hovered around the Trotskyist

5. A work that deals incisively with the psychological commonalities of the New Left inside and outside of the United States is Stanley Rothman, *The Roots of Radicalism: Jews, Christians, and the Left* (New Brunswick, N.J.: Transaction Publishers, 1996).

6. A collection of essays about German opponents of the German New Left who observe this boomerang effect of American reeducation is *Die 68er und ihre Gegner: Der Widerstand gegen die Kulturrevolution*, ed. Hartmuth Becker, Felix Dirsch, and Stefan Winckler (Graz: Leopold Stocker Verlag, 2003).

7. See Michael Kleeberg's essay in *Die Welt*, May 22, 1999.

organization Ligue Communiste and contributed to its publication *Rouge*. In commenting on the political evolution of today's journalistic titan Plenel, Bensaïd has remarked that he "had underestimated the point at which Edwy's commitment had carried him outside the workers' movement" into what became "cultural Trotskyism."[8]

■ Antifascism

The vehicle for this New Leftist engagement has been the European Socialist parties far more than the eroding European Communist ones. In France since 1972 Socialists and Communists had worked together as a leftist bloc, backing each other's candidates in runoff elections and agreeing on a "Common Program of the Left." Although the Communists had begun as the stronger of the two partners, by 1978 their vote totals had fallen, by more than two percentage points, behind those of the Socialists, a trend that would continue to grow in the succeeding two decades. Socialists simply adapted better to certain changes. Unlike the Communists, they grasped that electorates had to be constructed for each election, and that their own future was tied to a rising professional class, which was throwing away bourgeois Christian values, and to a growing North African immigrant population. At the same time, Communist leaders were trying to mediate between the immigrants, whom they hoped would eventually return home to spread Marxism, and their working-class constituency. By the end of the twentieth century, the PCF had fallen between two stools, seeing what remained of the *classe ouvrière* drift toward the Front National of Jean Le Pen while the North African vote went increasingly to the Socialists.[9]

Equally important, the Socialist parties in Western Europe have begun to mimic Communist idiosyncrasies, thereby creating the appearance of continuity between the old CPs and themselves. Since the electoral alliance in 1972 between Communist and So-

8. Pierre Péan and Philippe Cohen, *La face cachée du monde: Du contre-pouvoir aux abus de pouvoir* (Paris: Mille et Une Nuits, 2003), 45–65, quote on 47.

9. Lavabie and Platone, *Que reste-t-il du PCF?* 64–67.

cialist heads Georges Marchais and François Mitterrand, the French Socialists had avoided criticizing Communist governments and their repressive politics. Thus when the Communist press in 1973, led by Marchais, went after Alexander Solzhenitsyn for exposing Soviet crimes, as a fascist and enemy of détente, Mitterrand and the Socialist party paper *L'Unité* avoided saying anything that would offend their pro-Soviet partners. By 1975, however, *L'Unité* was publishing attacks on Solzhenitsyn's "impassive peasant face" and lack of social compassion that seems to have been extracted from the Communist *L'Humanité*.[10] In this case, as the French say, *"l'appétit vient en mangeant."*

Socialist efforts at appeasing the Communists is the customary explanation as to why Jospin would not admit that Stalin had committed mass murder, when in November 1997 he responded as premier to questions in the French National Assembly concerning the Soviet past. The bone of contention that day was *Le livre noir du communisme* published by Stéphane Courtois, a catalogue of Communist crimes throughout the world compiled by a moderate leftist critic of Communist systems. Courtois pleaded with the French Left to come clean about the record of leftist totalitarianism.[11] The view proposed by *Le Monde,* that Jospin praised Communist antifascism and scorned any "attempt at equivalence between Stalinist and fascist crimes" out of deference to his Communist allies, does not work. This explanation has been randomly extended to every Socialist leader in Europe who has denied that Communist regimes have something to atone for. It ignores the effect of ideological changes in recent decades among European Socialists. Their unwillingness to acknowledge the extent of Communist wrongdoing expresses itself in other defensive habits, such as the ascription of base motives to Communist critics, a practice that stretches back among Communists to the campaigns against Kravchenko and Solzhenitsyn. Supposedly those who notice Communist crimes are trying to divert attention from other atrocities produced by the Right, particularly the Holocaust. This catastrophe, which the Post-Marxist Left is instrumentalizing, without

10. *L'Unité,* feature essay, January 24, 1975.

11. Stéphane Courtois, Nicolas Wert, et al., *Le livre noir du communisme* (Paris: Robert Laffont, 1997).

protest from European Jewish organizations, is blamed on the
Frankfurt School's customary demons: Christians, nationalists,
and anti-immigrationists have all been assigned places in the antecedents or progress of fascist ideology.[12]

The attempted linkage between excuses for the Communist past
and the exigencies of parliamentary alliances exaggerates the coalition value of disintegrating Communist parties. The Communists
require Socialist allies to be included in coalitions far more than
vice versa. In Germany outside of Berlin, leftist coalitions can easily operate without the Communist Party now reconstructed as
the PDS; nonetheless, the Socialists and Greens persist in playing
the role of Communist fellow-travelers, trivializing Communist
crimes, calling for amnesty for former Communist secret police
and stressing the need to overcome Germany's "fascist past." In
France the Communists and in Italy the successor parties to the
PCI have been more candid than the Socialists in admitting to
Communism's dark side. As apologists for or disguisers of this
historical record, the non-Communist Left, composed of Socialists and Greens, hold pride of place. European Socialists were
ironically for the most part unwavering in their support of the
anti-Communist side during the Cold War.

Such behavior might be explained by looking at the dominant
themes of the Post-Marxist Left. This Left models itself on certain Communist practices, by fighting perpetually against "fascism" and by promoting revolution, now reinterpreted as cultural
upheaval. *Le Monde,* in its book section, "Le Monde des Livres,"
awards good or bad grades to authors in terms of whether they
reflect what one critic calls the "cultural Trotskyist" grid.[13] The
paper's editorial board openly supports the suppression of ideas
held to be insensitive or else reminiscent of the Vichy past and of
the "collabos" who participated in the Vichy government. The
Loi Gayssot, introduced in July 1990 by a Communist deputy
and overwhelmingly endorsed by the Socialists, sets out to punish
délits d'opinion, criminal acts that consist of denying the Nazi
Holocaust or expressing hateful remarks about religious and ethnic
groups. This law was designed and has been applied to prevent or

12. Annie Kriegel, "Le leurre de l'antisémitisme," *Le Figaro,* April 2, 1990, 2.
13. Péan and Cohen, *Face cachée,* 513–39.

inhibit criticism of immigration, the growing Islamicist presence in France, and responses to attacks on the French Catholic identity.[14] *Le Monde, Libération, Le Point, Nouvel Observateur,* and much of the rest of the French press advocate that reactionary ideas be suppressed, and Center-Left coalitions throughout Western and Central Europe have introduced legislation similar to the Loi Gayssot. In July 1993, *Le Monde,* at the urging of Plenel, published above the names of academic and journalistic celebrities, including Italian semanticist and novelist Umberto Eco, an "Appeal to Vigilance," directed against the "red-brown" alliance that is allegedly threatening European democracy. The signatories expressed concern that unless muzzled, this growing opposition to a multicultural France, comprised of the dissident Left and the nationalist Right, would endanger the society that progressives were trying to build.[15]

"Cultural Trotskyism" may be a suitable description of this Left, which is actuated by a vision of perpetual cultural change and bureaucratically contrived social engineering. Neither a working-class consciousness nor socialist economic planning is considered necessary to advance this leftist agenda. In France it entails a war being waged on those deemed insufficiently multicultural or those imagined to be connected spiritually to the Vichy "fascist" regime. A mass publication in France that has criticized this politics of denunciation, *Le Figaro-Magazine* has observed how the French press and intelligentsia drag designated collaborators "out of their coffins each day and shoot them again and again. It is no longer a question of nuances. Here are the human filth and ordure who failed to resist fascism; here are the collaborators." A Jewish scholar of Heidegger, Alain Finkielkraut, in a comment in *Le Figaro-Magazine,* announced that he deplores this antifascist "Manichean vision," which "replaces a political understanding of the world by means of a simplistic moral dualism." Possibly surpassing in

14. A detailed critical discussion of the Loi Gayssot can be found in Eric Delcroix's *La police de la pensée contre le révisionnisme* (Paris: Diffusion, 1994); for a glowing defense of the same legislation, see Christian Delacompagne, "La tolérance et ses limites," in *La philosophie politique aujourd'hui: Idées, débats, enjeux* (Paris: Seuil, 2000), 34–56.

15. See Elisabeth Lévy, *Les maîtres censeurs* (Paris: Jean Claude Lattes, 2002), 129–70.

vulgarity even Nazi rhetoric, the cultural Trotskyists and antifascists have reduced political discourse to a "medical, biological vocabulary of eradication."[16] Thus the French radical socialist but critic of national disintegration Jean-Pierre Chevènement has been denounced as savagely in the French leftist press as has the conservative nationalist Le Pen. His expressed anxiety about declining French natality has caused the center-left publication *L'Express* (February 1, 1996) to accuse Chevènement of "harboring nationalist nostalgia that exudes the fumes of the family values of yesteryear."[17] His appeal to French workers against the European Union and his endorsement of Swedish socialists, who have provided state subsidies to women wishing to have families, we are told, is a "pretext for antifeminism." Although an economic socialist, Chevènement is accused of being an undeclared member of the "red-brown" conspiracy organized against multiculturalism.[18]

The leftist weekly *Libération* has been waging a battle since 1979, which it treats as integral to Marxism, for legal and social acceptance of homosexual lifestyles and even of pederasty. In a dossier on gay pride published on June 26, 1999, *Libération* presented the war against homophobia as essential to the leftist struggle against fascism: "Homophobia, the offspring of the evil beast that is born of racism, requires our continuing vigilance." Dealing with it will take persistent efforts "not only in the battle for expanded rights but also in the realm of human emotions, in an area that has already been corrupted by the established culture and by political symbols."[19] A kind of guilt by association operates in several editorials published in *Le Monde* in 2000 about a plan to rebury the remains of nineteenth-century French composer Hector Berlioz in the Paris Panthéon. Since Berlioz had based his opera *Les Troyens* on Virgil's *The Aeneid*, a Roman epic that celebrates Latin antiquities, honoring Berlioz would be tantamount to glorifying Mussolini and his brand of Latin fascism. Such a move, *Le Monde* seems to be arguing by quoting the ad-

---

16. *Le Figaro-Magazine*, April 10, 1998, 18.

17. Sévillia, *Le terrorisme*, 214–61.

18. Bernard-Henri Lévy, "Chevènement–Le Pen, même combat," *Le Monde*, April 8, 1999.

19. Gérard Lefort, "Le réveil homophobe," *Libération*, June 27, 1999, 49.

monitions of Jean Kahn, Philippe Olivier, and Gottfried Wagner, should be reconsidered, particularly when decent people are battling fascist residues. An "act of extreme gravity," reburying Berlioz, which has now been postponed, is linked in *Le Monde* to another ominous prospect, allowing Berlioz's music dealing with European national antiquities to be played in European concert halls.[20]

This Post-Marxist style of imprecation now in vogue treats European, but not Third World, national pride as manifestations of "Pétainisme," "Nazism," or Holocaust denial. Thus a book by French sociologist Paul Yonnet, *Voyage au centre du malaise français*, which analyzes the loss of national identity in his country, comes under attack in *Le Monde* and *Nouvel Observateur* for ignoring the crimes of the Vichy regime.[21] Those who are dissatisfied with the evanescence of French national sentiment are supposedly justifying at least indirectly the Nazi deportation of Jews carried out in Paris in 1942. German Nazis and their French collaborators are somehow benefiting from Yonnet's sociology in a way that is never convincingly explained. Other such emotional connections are becoming the order of the day outside of France. Both German Socialists and the German national press have gone after the sponsors of a plan for creating in Berlin a center for commemorating postwar German refugees, on the grounds that these commemorators are slighting the Holocaust. The same is true of others who call attention to politically incorrect objects of study, such as the Allied saturation bombing of German cities between 1943 and the end of the Second World War and the mass rape of German and Eastern European women by the Soviet armies moving westward in 1945.[22] Any focusing on unpleasant acts that targeted Germans or were committed by the Soviets must conceal the intention to

20. See the quoted remarks in response to the inquiry in *Le Monde*, June 21, 2000; and the ultra-Jacobin attack on Berlioz by Joël-Marie Fauquet, "Berlioz au Panthéon? Une fausse note," ibid., February 29, 2000.

21. Paul Yonnet, *Voyage au centre du malaise français* (Paris: Gallimard, 1993); "Sur la crise du lien national," *Le Débat* (May–August 1993), 132–43; Jean-Marie Colombani, review of *Voyage au centre du malaise français*, in *Le Monde*, February 5, 1993, 27; and Jean-Claude Maurin, "Fièvre épuratrice dans l'intelligensia," *Eléments* 108 (April 2003), 35–43.

22. See Heinz Nawratil, *Der Kult mit der Schuld: Geschichte im Unterbewussten* (Munich: Universitas, 2002), 1–43.

commit Holocaust revision. What is legally banned may be less important than what is disallowed politically and journalistically.

The Post-Marxist Left is not without sympathy for American ideals and even for capitalism. When the United States intervened against Serbia in 1999, European leftist intellectuals extolled American power and went after those who questioned the motives for American intervention. *Le Monde* and *Libération* criticized opponents of the NATO aerial attacks on Serbia as *Pétainistes* and, playing on semantic associations with Holocaust denial, complained about the eruption of *révisionnisme*. By the late nineties, as Elisabeth Lévy shows exhaustively in *Les maîtres censeurs,* pro-American sentiment was so powerful among the French intelligentsia that Bernard-Henri Lévy, Pascal Bruckner, and the editorial board of *Le Monde* routinely applied the "right-wing extremism" label to any critic of American imperialism.[23] It would be wrong to trace this attitude to support for the Muslim Bosnians pitted against the Christian Serbs in Kosovo exclusively. Although European multiculturalists saw the struggle against Serbia as a path leading toward a new Europe built on human rights doctrines, their pro-American feeling went deeper.

The U.S. government was showered with praise from the European Left in 2000 for sending dire warnings to the Austrian government, which was considering a coalition that would include the right-wing Österreichische Freiheitspartei and its controversial head, Jorg Haider. At that point the United States was seen as taking a leadership role in the antifascist front being mounted by European Socialist coalitions and the European Union.[24] It was the United States that insisted that any Eastern European state that wished to join NATO would have to integrate into its public education a prescribed program of study on the Holocaust. Small wonder that one of *Le Monde*'s senior editors, Alain Minc, explained last year "no democrat can ever be anti-American, seeing that America is the land identified in an almost ontological sense

---

23. Jean-Christophe Rufin, *La dictature libérale* (Paris: Lattès, 1994); and Lévy, *Les maîtres censeurs*, 278–91. Lévy writes about "the orphans of Marxism in search of a substitute faith contributing significantly to the victory of a globalized neoliberalism, which is the new visage of Reason in history and of a universal hope" (ibid., 158).

24. Gottfried, *Multiculturalism,* 104–10.

with modernity and progress."[25] Moreover, in 2002 *Le Monde* recommended Jean-François Revel's book-length defense of American power and extended attack on "anti-Americanism," *Europe's Anti-American Obsession.* Contrary to a settled opinion among Revel's American neoconservative sponsors, his polemic was certainly not treated with uniform contempt in the "anti-American" French press. Roger-Pol Droit, in a review for *Le Monde,* agreed with Revel that American power worked as the icebreaker of economic progress and globalization throughout the world. Revel had "redeemed the honor of intellectuals" by pointing out truths that needed to be heard.[26]

The United States is also extolled for destroying the Old Europe by exporting a new social economic model. Given the choice between full-dress socialism and a mixed consumerist economy that brings a less nationalistic and more culturally open Europe, prominent European leftists have moved steadily into the second camp. Alain Minc, former French president François Mitterrand, and architect of the Maastricht Treaties and the European Union Jacques Delors are prominent Socialists who have rejected the identification of their party with fixed economics or "dogma"—as opposed to an unceasing march into the future. Critics of this "avancisme" note that Socialists in government have lost interest in massive redistributions of income or in nationalizing production but view bureaucratic rule and markets as necessary for a world of "unlimited possibilities."[27]

It would be shortsighted to see in this nothing more than American consumerism decked out as "human rights." Those present-day leftists seeking a compromise with capitalism are often thinking people, like Giorgio Napolitano, the Italian Communist who in 1994 reorganized the PCI as the Democratic Party of the Left. Today this former Communist serves as an economic advisor to the European Parliament, after being the occupant of numerous other posts in this body. Both Napolitano and Delors have

---

25. Alain Minc, introduction to *Epîtres à nos nouveaux maîtres* (Paris: Grasset, 2003), 2–4. The tone of these letters is generally adulatory, despite Minc's references to American empire building.

26. Feature essay in *Le Monde des Livres, Le Monde,* September 13, 2002.

27. See Jacques Delors, introduction to *L'union politique de l'Europe* (Paris: Documentations Françaises, 1998).

reinterpreted socialism as something leading toward a bureaucratically administered future, free of national borders and of the
longtime Socialist "psychoanalytic complex about capitalism."[28]
By the time of the fall of the Soviet bloc, Napolitano was changing
ships in more than one way. His book *Europa, America dopo l'89*
(1992) makes clear that whatever attachment the author had once
felt toward the Soviet model was being transferred to the transatlantic victor of the Cold War.[29] The American example would
aid in the task of European integration, a process designed to bring
about a pluralistic, secularist social democratic European continent.

It is hard to make sense of this ideological transformation without noting the American presence. For many Europeans the
United States has become a hegemonic power socioeconomically,
culturally, and politically. It is the unavoidable reference point by
which they grasp their place in the world and by which the Post-
Marxist Left is charting its future. A comparison that comes to
mind is how the Greek world looked at Sparta from its victory in
the Peloponnesian War in 404 B.C. until its defeat at the hands of
the Thebans at Leuctra thirty-three years later. Athenian historians
and philosophers, including Plato, Thucydides, and Xenophon,
the last of whom requested and received Spartan citizenship, held
up the moderation, thrift, and bravery of the Spartans as worthy
of imitation by other Greeks. The oligarchs who established themselves in Athens's defeated maritime democracy after the Peloponnesian War accepted as their slogan the characteristically Spartan ideal of *sophrosunē* (moderation), and imitations of the then
decayed Spartan constitution sprang up in other Greek societies.
The military disaster that Sparta suffered while trying to invade
its rival Thebes and its subsequent loss of conquered territory in
Messenia (in the Peloponnesus) led to a loss of prestige and influence from which it never recovered.

What makes the United States decidedly different is the far
greater scale of its influence and hegemony, beside which ancient
military empires, including Rome, pale by comparison. Europeans
have taken over American ideals and practices despite the peri-

28. See Delors's remarks in *Le Monde*, October 4, 2003.

29. Giorgio Napolitano, *Europa, America dopo l'89* (Rome: Laterza, 1992);
Leonardo Raito, *USA and Eurocommunism in the Age of the Cold War* (Baton
Rouge: Louisiana State University Press, 2002).

odic ritual of castigating American arrogance. America's European critics with few exceptions are not calling for a nationalist, monarchist, or anti–welfare state regime in place of the supranational, bureaucratic, and pluralistic order associated with the United States. More common criticisms from the European Left are that the United States has not gone far enough to honor its "human rights" or pluralistic ideals and that it does not consult Europe often enough before applying military power.

One relation between these Western centers explored in my book *Multiculturalism and the Politics of Guilt* is the delayed acceptance by European governments of social policies initiated in the United States. Immigration reform for the benefit of Third World populations, followed by laws aimed at curbing discrimination against racial minorities and recognition of feminist and gay rights, began in the United States about ten to fifteen years earlier than in Western Europe. France is now moving in the direction of "positive discrimination" for racial-ethnic minorities, according to its interior minister, Nicolas Sarkozy.[30] This policy the United States initiated in the late sixties and early seventies has found champions in the (right-of-center) French government thirty years later. Whereas some multicultural experiments have taken a more extreme form in Europe, as in the criminalization of insensitive opinions, they have usually been introduced after similar developments had been put into effect across the Atlantic. With few if any exceptions, the American press has seconded the harsh measures that Europeans are applying to deal with insensitivity. American journalists remind their readers of Europe's "fascist" past and of the fact that in Germany the Allied High Command began the process of banning "undemocratic" views to cleanse the country of nationalist thinking. In any case the American press will not likely take up the cudgels for badly treated French or German "right-wing" authors.[31]

30. Gottfried, *Multiculturalism*, 72–109; Sophie Huet, "La discrimination positive ne fait pas recette," *Le Figaro*, November 25, 2003, 1. See also the online protest letter by the son of a French worker, *"D'ascendance européenne,"* or contact@jeunesses-identitaires.com.

31. For a sympathetic treatment of the decision by Belgian courts to ban the largest party in Flanders for its anti-immigration stands, see Angus Roxborough, "Blow to Belgian Far Right," on www.newsvote.bbc.co.uk (November

There is presently only one newsworthy group on the European left, Attac, with about eighty thousand members worldwide, that actively opposes the economic globalization identified with the United States. An umbrella organization for old Marxists and anticapitalist ecologists, this group prides itself on its capacity to grab headlines by staging demonstrations in Genoa, Seattle, and other cities in which the major economic powers are meeting.[32] Such activists dismiss the European parliamentary Left as having no interest in world economic redistribution or in dispossessing multinational corporations. In point of fact, the Post-Marxist Left—from England's New Labourites to such continental blocs as the Italian Party of the Democratic Left, the French Socialist-Communist coalition, the German Social Democrats, and the PDS—does not show interest in making common cause with the antiglobalist Left. And while the Greens have appropriated scraps of its invective, they too are now part of a Post-Marxist parliamentary alliance and express its worldview. In this thematic and programmatic shift, revolutionary economic change has taken a backseat to an ideology of open borders, gay rights, and feminism.

Another point that requires rectification is the contrast sometimes drawn between an increasingly radicalized Europe and a relatively conservative American society. Except for a more sharply falling birth rate and stiffer penalties for politically incorrect statements, Western Europe reveals the same general cultural and social trends as the United States. Despite their special pleading for the left wing of the Democratic Party, Thomas Ferguson and Joel

---

9, 2004). In the annual reports by agencies designed to protect the German constitutional order, established by the Allied Command, "anti-American" and "constitutionally hostile" have become interchangeable phrases. See, for example, the *Verfassungsschutz Berichte des Bundes* (1998), 97; (1999), 74. On how German "constitutionality" has become synonymous with multiculturalism and support for "American values," see Josef Schüsslburner's pamphlet "Kampfinstrument: Antisemitismus-Vorwurf: Vom Verfassungsschutz zur Staatsreligion" (Berlin: Friedenskomitee, 2000). On the Nuremberg Trials, from the American perspective, see Eugene Davidson, *The Trial of the Germans* (reprint, Columbia: University of Missouri Press, 1997).

32. For a sympathetic treatment of Attac by a German conservative nationalist formerly on the anticapitalist left, see Werner Olles, "Die Aktualität der Linken," in *Junge Freiheit*, January 9, 2004, 18.

Rogers, in *Right Turn,* bring up serious questions about shifting American social attitudes in the eighties. Polling data indicate that most American citizens were not drifting rightward in this period, an opinion frequently encountered then and now among historians and social commentators.[33] Despite their Republican votes, Americans were not assenting to a "conservative Reagan revolution," but supporting a party in power that seemed to be managing things well. If Ferguson and Rogers are correct, the eighties in the United States were a decade of leftward movement on feminist, minority, and family issues. The population and culture were moving in this direction, no matter how the media depicted the government.

A book by Larry Schwab, *The Illusion of a Conservative Reagan Revolution,* presents a more far-reaching and less tendentious argument than *Right Turn* by demonstrating how little President Reagan changed social programs inherited from his Democratic predecessor. Schwab concludes on the basis of his evidence that there was "no Reagan conservative revolution" save for certain rhetorical assurances to the faithful.[34] On rights for women and minorities and on abortion, the country in the eighties was moving leftward in sentiment; and despite having a president who appealed to patriotism, the government did little to stop this current or to cut social programs drastically. Nor is it correct to assume that outside of more extensive welfare state programs, Europe has lunged further leftward than the United States. While some European countries have introduced governmentally subsidized day-care centers and most have socialized medicine, Europe has been less, not more, pluralistic than the United States. Europeans, for example, have not permitted anything approaching the present American Third World immigration rate. In the United States it is the "globalist" Right as much as the multicultural Left that has championed Third World immigration and supported the amnesty-ing of illegal aliens.

33. Thomas Ferguson and Joel Rogers, *Right Turn: The Decline of the Democrats and the Future of American Politics* (New York: Hill and Wang, 1986), 16–24, 193–96.

34. Larry M. Schwab, *The Illusion of a Conservative Reagan Revolution* (New Brunswick, N.J.: Transaction Publishers, 1991).

■ The Habermasian Moment

Among spokesmen for the Post-Marxist Left, Jürgen Habermas may well be the most prominent and in his own country the most honored. An advocate of "militant" democracy since the 1950s, he has defended his persuasion in the international press, in multiple books and articles, and as an academic lecturer. Habermas proclaims himself to be the proud heir of the American reeducation of the Germans that took place after the war. Despite his rise in the Hitlerjugend, a distinction shared with other scholars who have been equally intent on breaking with the German past, Habermas by the early fifties had moved into the anti-German Left. He regarded what the Germans had suffered during and after the war as fully deserved and spoke of his country's unconditional surrender as a "liberating experience."[35]

Notwithstanding his reputation as a socialist and as an apologist for the Communist German Democratic Republic, Habermas has been reticent about a program of sweeping economic reconstruction for the West Germans. His first major publication, which came out in *Merkur* in 1954, "Die Dialektik der Rationalisierung," was an extended critique of consumerism that incorporated themes from the antimodernist Right as well as from the Frankfurt School. This commentary took aim at advanced industrial societies for refusing to "place limits on technical organization in order to permit natural and social forces to express themselves."[36] Although Habermas's early work reprises the theme of "alienation" found in the young Marx, it also makes references to Martin Heidegger's

35. On Habermas's greater tendency to assign collective guilt to the German people for their authoritarian past than was evident in the older generation of the Critical Theorists, see Wiggershaus, *Theodor W. Adorno*, 135–38. In *Adorno: Eine politische Biographie,* Jäger makes the point that by the time of his death in 1969, Adorno had carried his "anticapitalist negativity" as far as he could. Others would adapt his method to new objects of attack. In Habermas's case, Adorno's repugnance for nations as "anachronisms that are resistant to Reason" would take the form of an ethic of German self-rejection. Habermas's association with the Hitlerjugend, an experience he shared with two other outspokenly Teutonophobic historical scholars, Fritz Fischer and Walter Jens, contributed to this propensity.

36. Jürgen Habermas, "Die Dialektik der Rationalisierung: Vom Pauperismus in Produktion und Konsum," *Merkur* 8, no. 8 (1954), 701–24.

existential philosophy and to Arnold Gehlen's sociobiological examination of human institutions. (Both these points of reference in Germany at the time were clearly associated with the German national right though not necessarily with the Nazis.) The influence in Habermas's early commentary of Adorno's and Horkheimer's *Dialectic of the Enlightenment* is too obvious to be ignored and surely impressed one graying radical. Soon after the publication of this essay, Adorno invited Habermas, who was then finishing graduate studies at Göttingen, to join him as a collaborator at the reestablished Institute for Social Research in Frankfurt. The main thrust of Habermas's youthful essay was to focus on industrial affluence as a form of "compensation" for human self-alienation. What the work teaches is that "consumption is being turned into a substitute for what humans lose as a result of technical progress."[37]

But such cultural observations, whether or not true, do not necessarily lead into socialist projects. A long evaluation of political attitudes among German university students, framed by his introduction, that Habermas helped Adorno put together in 1957, has few recognizably socialist prescriptions. Although abounding in moral righteousness and praise for the American reeducation of his countrymen, which Habermas suggests did not go far enough, *Student und Politik* only touches on economics tangentially, by venting disdain on moneyed interests for standing in the way of political equality. Habermas castigates German students for not being sufficiently attuned to social justice and in many cases voting for the center-right Christian Democrats; nonetheless, it is not clear what kind of economic revamping he had in mind for removing a hated capitalist past. Habermas laments the mediating role played by state bureaucrats in a defective German democracy, but he neglects to come up with other, more "democratic" organizational forms that might change this situation.

Most important is the emphasis he places on evaluating student responses in a way that might show who is "democratic" or who is "authoritarian." Only 171 respondents participated in the survey originally done for *Student und Politik*, a figure that two

---

37. Ibid., 723; Wiggershaus, *Die Frankfurter Schule*, 601–3.

years later, after heavy criticism, was expanded to 550. Despite the apparent preponderance of those who endorsed democratic institutions, of the fifty-two respondents initially classified as having democratic tendencies, only six, by Habermas's most demanding standards, were classed as impeccably democratic.[38] When students were reexamined on the basis of "democratic and authoritarian potentials," as viewed by Habermas and his coinvestigators, only 9 percent were thought to exhibit a "democratic disposition"—as opposed to 16 percent who were assigned an authoritarian one. Both the ideologically colored understanding of the key terms and the unwillingness to allow empirical facts to guide the investigation raise questions about the survey's value. Indeed, Horkheimer quarreled with Adorno about whether to publish this study under the institute's aegis, a difference that grew even more intense when in 1958 Habermas hoped to replace philosophy with a historical view aimed at reforming popular consciousness along socialist lines. Habermas raised the need for a "revolutionary change" in the public's perception of democracy as a preliminary step toward moving beyond the "bourgeois" foundation of the German Federal Republic.[39]

But these desired changes pertained to a transformation of consciousness more than economic revolution and, according to intellectual historian Ernst Topitsch, had little to do with empirical proofs. In Frankfurt School fashion, Habermas dismisses the accumulated observations and research data that do not fit his social programs as mere "positivism." By the sixties, what shaped his critical commentary were the avoidance of empiricism, the Left's identification with moral purity, and the demand that Germans atone for their fascist past. In his essay "Dogmatismus, Vernunft und Entscheidung," Habermas dwells on the unacceptable costs of living and thinking with "scientific method." This fate blinds us to the "relation between theory and practice that relates to the tradition of great philosophy and to a good, proper, and true

38. This text was printed in the series *Soziologische Texte*, ed. Heinz Maus (Berlin: Luchterhand Verlag, 1961).
39. This argument pervades Habermas's book *Strukturwandel der Öffentlichkeit: Untersuchung zu einer Kategorie der bürgerlichen Gesellschaft* (Berlin: Neuwied, 1962), a work originally submitted as a *Habilitationsschrift* at the University of Frankfurt.

communal life for individuals and citizens."[40] Even more relevant, this "scientization of our society" impedes our freedom; for "the experience of emancipation requires critical insight into power relations whose objectivity continues to be accepted until we can see through these relations." In place of empirical investigation, Habermas calls for a "theory" predicated on "experience" or "practice," a form of "communicative activity" *(kommunikatives Handeln)* that clarifies questions and brings about "understanding" *(Verständigung)*.[41] But the consequences of this turn are never fully clarified. Once cut adrift from the methods of investigation he rejects, explains German philosopher of science Gerard Radnitzky, Habermas is forced to anchor his "theory" in his own privileged conscience.[42]

In the next thirty years, he looked for a fit between the view of moral reason taught by Immanuel Kant, as a behavioral compass operating independently of empirical circumstances, and depth psychology. Habermas talked about rationally formed moral rules, while pointing grimly to the irrational causes of social behavior. What was irrational is apparently what did not correspond to his sense of democratic reform. At the same time, he adorned his conception of "communal understanding" with what Topitsch considers a religious mystical element. It is one that Habermas might have taken from his German Pietist ancestors, who had settled near his birthplace in Gummersbach in northwest Germany. Although Habermas does try to distance himself and his hypothetical community of rational speakers from Christian metaphysics, as Topitsch correctly notes, he presents a social drama centered on a fall from grace and a quest for redemption.[43] He speaks about

---

40. Ernst Topitsch, *Im Irrgarten der Zeitgeschichte: Ausgewählte Aufsätze* (Berlin: Duncker & Humblot, 2003), 93–130; Jürgen Habermas, "Dogmatismus, Vernunft und Entscheidung: Zu Theorie und Praxis in der verwissenschaftlichten Zivilisation," in *Theorie und Praxis* (Berlin: Neuwied, 1963), 243.

41. Habermas's plea for a "nonscientific" communicative method is first fully revealed in "Gegen einen positivistisch halbierten Rationalismus: Erwiderung eines Pamphlets," in *Kölner Zeitschrift für Soziologie und Sozialpsychologie* (1964), 336–59.

42. Gerard Radnitzky, "Im Irrgarten der Zeitgeschichte: Ernst Topitsch— ein Leben im Dienste der Aufklärung," *Aufklärung und Kritik* (August 2004), 45–46.

43. Topitsch, *Im Irrgarten der Zeitgeschichte*, 93–130.

how "positivism, historicism, and pragmatism each breaks loose under the impact of science being reduced to the productive force of an industrial society. A particularized reason is brought down to the level of subjective consciousness, whether as the power to verify hypotheses empirically or as historical understanding, or as a pragmatic social constraint. A disinfected reason has been cleansed of enlightened volition and has emptied itself of its own life. And this despiritualized but haunted life becomes an arbitrary one once it seeks to make decisions."[44]

Habermas offers himself as the spiritual guide for those brought to this pass, but since as the privileged framer of "democratic" discourse, he is also allowed to violate its first rule. The intended discourse is to be *herrschaftsfrei*, without one participant cowing another, yet this stated procedure does not keep Habermas from cutting down dissenters. In 1986 during the "historians' controversy," German historians Ernst Nolte, Michael Stürmer, Andreas Hillgruber, and Rainer Zitelmann undertook to "contextualize" the Nazi period in ways that displeased Habermas. These scholars expressed the view that the Nazi oppression of Jews and Hitler's invasion of the Soviet Union had to be understood against the background of interwar German reactions to Communist violence. Middle-class Europeans, and particularly Germans, felt threatened by Communist revolution, which they associated with Soviet mass murder. They also noticed the disproportionately high rate of Jews involved in Communist rule, including the operation of the Soviet secret police. All of these associations made them ripe for a dictatorship that declared war on Communism and international Jewry.[45]

Prescinding from the question of historical accuracy, which does not seem to enter into Habermas's discourse, we might note his heated efforts to exorcise the new "revisionism." Between 1987 and 1990 he explained in a series of attacks that these "revision-

44. Jürgen Habermas, *Erkenntnis und Interesse,* 2d ed. (Frankfurt am Main: Suhrkamp, 1969), 239.

45. See Ernst Nolte, *Der europäische Bürgerkrieg* (Berlin: Propyläen, 1987); "Die Ausschau nach dem Ganzen: Wissenschaftliches Ethos und Historisierung," *Frankfurter Allgemeine Zeitung,* July 18, 1987; *Abschliessende Reflexionen über den sogenannten Historikerstreit,* ed. Uwes Backes, Eckhardt Jesse, and Rainer Zitelmann (Berlin: Propyläen, 1990), 83–135.

ists" had "dangerously" equated Stalin's crimes with those of Hitler. They had thereby lapsed into what he called an "*Aufrechnungsansatz*," diverting attention to Communist crimes in order to play down German iniquity. Such ideas went against the "reeducation" that the Germans had enjoyed during the Allied Occupation but which the avoidable catastrophe of the Cold War had then interrupted. Although Habermas did not call for a total prohibition on the expression of such views, he insisted they should be confined to "specialized scientific journals" that would not reach the public.[46] Topitsch makes the point that his own first publication, a study of Thucydides that included barbed references to the Third Reich, came out in an arcane journal that Germany's totalitarian government had not bothered to close down.[47]

A historian of the antinationalist Left, Immanuel Geiss, reacted to Habermas's warnings with obvious irritation: "For someone who runs around lecturing to the rest of us about discourses, political culture, and enlightenment, one would expect him to show at least minimal respect for the conditions without which neither democracy nor science can survive. Rarely has a philosopher so thoroughly contradicted himself as Habermas did during this historians' controversy."[48] Although Geiss deserves praise for his valorous defense of intellectual freedom, Habermas was not behaving inconsistently when he excluded unwelcome debate. Never does he claim that he wants exactly those liberal freedoms that Geiss has in mind. Nor is he dedicated to any traditional process of verification applied in the physical and natural sciences. Habermas's method is to accord legitimacy to communicative activities that he considers properly "emancipating" and which are conducive to regret over Germany's tortured history.

As a discussion leader he is prodding his presumed participants back toward the German reeducation that took place in the postwar

---

46. Jürgen Habermas, "Vom öffentlichen Gebrauch der Historie," in *Historikerstreit: Die Dokumentation der Kontroverse um die Einzigartigkeit der nationalsozialistischen Judenvernichtung*, ed. Rudolf Augstein (Munich: R. Piper, 1987), 243–45. For a less vitriolic criticism of Nolte's contextualization, see my detailed commentary, "Nolte on Heidegger," *Society* 30, no. 5 (August 1993), 88–93.

47. Topitsch, *Im Irrgarten der Zeitgeschichte*, 131–37.

48. See Immanuel Geiss's remarks in *Die Habermas Kontroverse: Ein deutscher Streit* (Berlin: Siedler Verlag 1988), 62.

years. This excludes any "contextualization" of Nazism that does not lead to the desired educational end. A false "contextualization" cannot encourage, from his way of thinking, a definitive break from the bourgeois or prebourgeois society that had made Nazi atrocities possible. (Whether or not what Habermas considers nice thinking can be causally demonstrated is beside the point.) Thus, in a reflection on the *Historikerstreit* in 1990, Habermas lashes out at the "neohistoricists" who had reconceptualized the Holocaust as being unwilling "to cooperate in the overcoming of the paralysis of political culture." Their conceptual defect was "a primitive trust in terms of history and tradition." But because of the Holocaust, "a conscious life is no longer possible without distrust toward continuities that assert themselves without being questioned and which receive their validity by being taken for granted."[49] What attracts attention here is how a debate about overlapping totalitarian systems can be made to yield an excuse for condemning scholars who do not want to "overcome the German past." Ernst Nolte responded to this charge that a refutation should demonstrate that his scholarship is wrong. It should not assault his character because he had failed to endorse someone else's political project.[50]

A final point concerns Habermas's references to "revisionist." His critics have argued that all structured quests for knowledge (what the Germans style *Wissenschaften*) require a continuing reexamination and may turn out to be false or only partially valid. It is doubtful that one can be a real scholar by the received standards without being open to, and even welcoming, the possibility of "revision." Why then should Habermas be treating scientific inquiry when applied to modern European history as an act of

---

49. Jürgen Habermas, *Die nachholende Revolution: Kleine, politische Schriften* (Frankfurt am Main: Suhrkamp, 1990), 149.

50. For Nolte's conclusive statement on Habermas and other hostile critics, see *Das Vergehen der Vergangenheit: Antwort an meine Kritiker im sogenannten Historikerstreit* (Berlin: Ullstein, 1987). Like Geiss and other historians who criticize Habermas's contributions to the *Historikersreit*, Nolte does not grasp how pitifully little the task of verification matters for Habermas. Driving political concerns, which have been recast as self-evident moral values, have taken the place of *wissenschaftliche Methode*. See Gottfried, *Multiculturalism*, 78–100; and Steffen Kailitz, *Die politische Deutungskultur im Spiegel des Historikerstreits* (Wiesbaden: Westdeutscher Verlag, 2001).

moral irresponsibility? There are two answers. One, Habermas explicitly rejects *Wissenschaft* unless it incorporates his interests, which are unmasking bourgeois manipulations of "public opinion" and rooting out elitist and nationalist attitudes. From the early fifties onward, he went to war against empirical methodology or any traditional means of filtering and verifying data that did not satisfy his political criteria. What he hoped to see achieved were the teaching of history with a "practical purpose" and discussion that would be centered on consensus among well-intentioned democrats. In short, there is no reason to attribute to him inconsistency because of his repugnance for historical revision.

Against the background of this Post-Marxist irrationalism, it might be instructive to look at like-minded Americans welcoming Habermas into the "project of building a community through intersubjective reason." Thus Berkeley professor David Hollinger applauds Habermas's work in Germany, which parallels that of Richard Rorty and Martin Jay in the United States, to move beyond ethnic division by universalizing " 'our' democratic egalitarian ethos through immanent critique and the expansion of 'human rights' culture as far as social circumstances permit it to spread."[51] The gray eminence of this blending of multiculturalism and human rights, Richard Rorty, finds much in Habermas to applaud but worries that their shared admirers might confuse their distinctive positions. Habermas goes too far in insisting that it is "essential to a democratic society that its self-image embody the universalism and some form of the rationalism of the Enlightenment. He thinks of his account of 'communicative reason' as a way of updating rationalism." Unlike Habermas, Rorty wishes to allow "non-universalist" and "poeticized" interests to coexist with rational universalism, albeit only as a strategy for dealing with one's finitude.[52]

In the end, however, Rorty no less than Habermas wishes to push humanity into "replacing both religious and philosophical accounts of a suprahistorical ground or an end-of-history convergence with a historical narrative about the rise of liberal institutions

51. David A. Hollinger, *Postethnic America: Beyond Multiculturalism* (New York: Basic Books, 1995), 115.

52. Richard Rorty, *Contingency, Irony, and Solidarity* (Cambridge: Cambridge University Press, 1989), 17.

and customs—the institutions and customs that were designed to diminish cruelty, make possible government by consent of the governed, and permit as much domination-free communication as possible to take place." Such a move requires a "shift from epistemology to politics," which the American pragmatist and socialist John Dewey would advocate but "from which Habermas hangs back." As a stubborn rationalist, Habermas would not give up "the transcendental moment of universal validity" to notice the historical process through which "liberals" must work to make their ideas prevail.[53]

Habermas is fortunate in his putative American critics, who happily hide his blemishes or else share them to such a degree that they no longer stand out. Neither a universal form of reasoning nor liberalism in the classical sense informs Habermas's didactic approach to evaluating facts. Believing, as he does, that people should be made to think politically like himself and that the discussion-masters have to set limits on "domination-free discourse," lest it stray into "non-universalist" opinions, Habermas shies away from genuinely independent thinking, non–politically correct rationality, or limited government. Whether or not these are the highest human goods, one might expect Habermas, who claims rhetorically to believe in them, to pay at least minimal attention to the practice of uncensored discourse. But like Rorty, he is overwhelmed by an obtrusive finality. The quest for an egalitarian community, stripped of national and ethnic pasts, does not incline either one of them toward open discussion. Guided democracy or democratic centralism may be the closest they can come to a "domination-free" exchange of opinions.

Two, *revision* is now a code word on the Post-Marxist left for being politically incorrect, which means expressing "fascist" ideas. It does not refer exclusively to those who challenge the established account of the Holocaust, but it has been extended to those who are transmitting a historical narrative that might weaken our resistance to "fascist" threats. Thus in France "revisionist" is routinely applied to those who dwell on Soviet crimes or who question the mounting charges made against ordinary (typically Catholic) French people as being active or at least acquiescent collabora-

53. Ibid., 68, 69, 82–84.

tors in the Vichy regime. Solzhenitsyn is classed as a "revisionist" author because he makes the Soviet experiment look bad and thereby undermines the case for a uniquely evil Nazism—and for a uniquely evil Right, or for what is considered the "Right" at a particular moment. The judgment of the Post-Marxist Left does not single out those who are denying Hitler's crimes. And it most certainly is not a factual refutation. It is a political theological assessment, which means that anyone presumed to be guilty will be kept out of polite company, and indeed, in a properly run progressive regime, could land up in jail or forced rehabilitation. The sometimes deafening enthusiasm Habermas and Adorno have shown for Communists as antifascist educators gives their game away completely.

A charge often coupled with "revisionism," "denying or understating" Nazi uniqueness *(Einzigartigkeit* or *Einmaligkeit)*, is something that hardly ever takes place.[54] This crime serves the Post-Marxist Left as an object of imprecatory rhetoric and as a plan for social reeducation. All atrocities are "unique" in the sense that they occur within individual contexts and feature specific malefactors and victims. Stating that particular massacres resemble each other or that one mass killing may have led to another one is an assertion that may be questioned or affirmed but does not negate the particularity of a specific atrocity. The German "revisionists" may well have carried the causal connection they highlight too far. But this methodological defect does not mean that these "revisionists" were "Holocaust deniers" or "Holocaust trivializers," in the manner of the Post-Marxist Left. That emerging Left has become a rallying point in Europe for those who deny

---

54. Radnitzky, "Im Irrgarten der Zeitgeschichte," 45, 46. This critical point is central to Rolf Kosiek, *Historikerstreit und Geschichtsrevision* (Tübingen: Gräbert Verlag, 1989), which explores the war against "historical revisionism" as thought control. In this polemical exchange, the "antifascists" draw fevered comparisons between politically incorrect scholarship and the crime of "Holocaust denial." Since one side appeals to historical-scientific ideals and the other to sentiments, particularly historical guilt and the preferential right of designated victims, there is no way that the opposed sides can meaningfully communicate. Those who invoke "historical science" may not always offer airtight proofs, but those who argue against them are stifling questions that are deemed to be ideologically unacceptable. See a discussion of this problem of noncommunication in Gottfried, *After Liberalism,* 1–19, 144.

the real human costs of Communism. And these deniers accuse those who complain about their double standard of not coming to terms with the right-wing past. By means of the "antifascist" card, Habermas and his devotees have been able to control what in today's Europe is becoming the only permissible political and moral conversation.

■ American-Style Reeducation

Habermas is correct, however, to view the American reeducation experiment, which went on in his country from May 1945 until the creation of the postwar German government in 1948–1949, as a model for his own engagement. It would not be too much to claim that this occupation included intimations of the Post-Marxist Left, at a time when political Marxism still raged among European intellectuals. A former chief theorist and board member of the German SDS, Bernd Rabehl, has pointed to the "substitutions for a lost radicalism" that onetime revolutionaries, including the German foreign minister, Joschka Fischer, have employed to keep radical change among the Germans alive. Having perceived the impossibility of an electoral leap into a Marxist-Leninist economy, these aging radicals have resorted to a cluster of taboos that "in a democracy can work in the same extreme fashion as classical radicalism." Towering over these taboos stand the twin evils of "fascism" and anti-Semitism, and to throttle all possible opposition to thought control, the taboo-wielders charge their critics with hoping to return to a evil past: "Instead of proceeding directly against German history, they clutter their collective past with taboos and destroy it as a culture-creating entity."[55]

Rabehl could have looked to the American occupation as the beginning of this process and, like Habermas, given credit to those who had helped establish the now prevalent taboos among his countrymen. Grouped around Major General Robert A. McClure, Eisenhower's advisor on psychological warfare and from early 1946 director of the Division of Information Control in Berlin,

---

55. Interview in Politikforum (www.politikforum.de/forum/archive/6/2004/06/01163689).

were those who made "democracy" synonymous with mind-manipulation. McClure's team, which determined who would be licensed to communicate news and ideas, teach in public institutions, and in some instances engage in commerce, did not include a single trained psychiatrist. His right-hand man, Murray I. Gurfein, had edited the *Harvard Law Review* and had been a longtime devotee of the Frankfurt School. The D of IC borrowed licensed psychiatrists from the British to put together their questionnaires for the personality tests applied over a three-year period.[56] The questionnaires bring to mind the tendentious research of Adorno and Habermas as they were looking for "authoritarian personalities." The investigations by McClure's assistants were intended to exclude "right-wing" personality types from entering public and professional life, and this exclusion would be extended to proven anti-Nazis, who were considered *reactionäre Widerständler,* anti-Communist anti-Nazis, avowed German patriots, or anyone associated with the landholding Prussian aristocracy.[57]

The most engaged opponents of the German past, typified by social psychologist Kurt Lewin, who assisted with the questionnaires, and secretary of the treasury Henry Morgenthau, advocated devastating economic measures. Borrowing from Morgenthau's plan for a defeated Germany in 1943, which was one of many overlapping plans then being formulated by American Teutonophobes, the hard-liners called for dismantling German industrial resources, which would be given to the Soviets; the worsening of inflation, which would generate prolonged scarcity; and the imposition of staggering reparations on a materially broken and bombed-out nation. Lewin, a social psychologist associated with the Frankfurt School, ardently favored all of these actions, in order

56. Among the works on this subject still available in English are C. J. Friedrich, *American Experience in Military Government in Germany* (Garden City, N.Y: Rhinehart, 1948); John Gimbel, *The American Occupation of Germany: Politics and the Military* (Stanford: Stanford University Press, 1968); W. E. Hocking, *Experiment in Education: What We Can Learn from Teaching Germany* (Chicago: University of Chicago Press, 1954); Marshall Knappen, *And Call It Peace* (Chicago: University of Chicago Press, 1947); E. H. Litchfield, *Governing Postwar Germany* (Ithaca: Cornell University Press, 1953).

57. See Caspar von Schrenck-Notzing, *Charakterwäsche: Die Politik der amerikanischen Umerziehung in Deutschland* (Munich: Kristall bei Langen Müller, 1981), 123–26.

to "achieve a total destruction of the forces that had kept the old order afloat." "Only chaos would enable a new elite to take over, once reactionary forces were liquidated." Moreover, "free market democrats are useless and it might be better to begin with outright reactionaries than to hope to build a new society with materially satiated half-democrats."[58]

Here the implicit belief that Germans were a tainted people coincided with the justification for the instructions given to Allied soldiers at the end of 1945 not to fraternize with those whose land they were occupying. These instructions dwelled on "the subterranean depths in which the fire of hatred, greed, and violence was flaring" and related this psychological problem to the entire course of German history. One had to remember "Nazism was not the product of a few extraordinary individuals but has deep roots in German civilization." The atrocities committed in Nazi concentration camps were not an aberration but were instead "typical of the Germans."[59]

The reeducation project continued to be pursued beyond the immediate postwar period. Although the Nuremberg Trials, which judged "Nazi war criminals," took place mostly in 1945 and 1946, the prosecutorial activity dragged on throughout the American occupation (which ended in 1955) and disinvestiture suits extended well into the late forties against those who were thought to have had too close an identification with the overthrown regime, such as I. G. Farben. Other cleansing devices continued to operate into the sixties and even later. "Denazification" investigations, which were set up to ascertain degrees of Nazi sympathy among those accused of having collaborated with Hitler's regime, went on throughout the American occupation.[60] Moreover, the Germans persisted in this process as a form of self-rehabilitation, once the Americans had more or less departed the political scene. They patrolled themselves relentlessly in terms of the educational materials that they allowed into their schools and that they judged acceptable for teaching the young. The German censuring authorities took measures to pulp *(Einstampfung)* or to remove from cir-

58. Ibid., 124.
59. Ibid., 185.
60. See the critical comments on this process of reeducation in Niall Ferguson, *Colossus: The Price of American Empire* (New York: Penguin, 2004), 72–74.

culation certain antidemocratic works. This practice is still in force in the German Republic, which destroys publications, whose distribution the government controls, in response to complaints about violated taboos. As a young German historian, Karl-Heinz Weissmann, has remarked about this hierarchy of prohibited themes and views, the ultimate taboo "is to prefer another civil religion to the one at whose center can be found the doctrine of collective guilt."[61]

Contrary to a now widespread supposition, German reeducation did not end with the onset of the Cold War. Certain things had changed by the late forties, including the once warm feelings toward Communist "antifascists" among the American occupants and the enforcement of a controlled economy intended to perpetuate German poverty in the Western occupation zones (all the Western zones were merged in 1946). The absence of overt Nazi sympathizers, the flooding of Germany with refugees from Eastern Europe, and the growth of the Soviet threat all worked to modify hostility toward the Germans. But what did not end despite these and other developments was a general commitment to alter German political culture to avoid a recrudescence of German nationalism.

It might be enlightening to look at the leftist sympathy that investigators and questionnaires associated with democratic loyalties. While those who framed the questions and typically favored a harsh peace were in some cases Communists or at least fellow travelers, they were not pushing the respondents into an avowal of Marxist-Leninist beliefs. Like Adorno and Habermas, they identified antifascism with a predilection for the Soviet regime and with a general dislike for bourgeois Christian society. What made the Communists a magnet for these investigators was the bourgeois adversary. That is to say, the Communists were seen as the enemies of their enemies, whose reactionary way of life had supposedly contributed to the victory of fascism.

The American sponsors of the reeducation were not all German Jewish radicals or Communist émigrés (despite the fact that

61. See the text of Weissmann's remarks in *Junge Freiheit*, May 28, 2004, 14; and Helmut Mosberg, *Reeducation: Umerziehung und Lizenzpresse im Nachkriegszeitdeutschland* (Munich: Universitas Verlag, 1991).

many of them were one or both). The theme of reeducation was not as strong among the other Western allies as among the Americans. For example, the Soviets cared far less about instilling democracy in the Germans than they did about dragging home war materiel, exploiting what remained of the German economy, and improving their geopolitical position in Central Europe. The plan for coerced uplift was quintessentially American and marked by that conversionary zeal that now animates the vision of bringing American democracy to the Middle East. The reeducation ambitions of social psychologists and political scientists like Harold Lasswell and Karl Lowenstein are not surprising, given the American enthusiasm for the yoking of the social sciences to the inculcation of "democratic" attitudes. And among the most fervent backers of enforced German reeducation were descendants of old-line WASP families, such as Major General McClure (1896–1973), poet Archibald MacLeish, political scientist Harold Lasswell, jurists Robert H. Jackson and Telford Taylor, philosopher John Dewey, and scion of the Wisconsin progressive family Charles La Follette. While these figures also mostly backed Roosevelt's social reforms, they were not for the most part particularly friendly toward the Soviets. But they did believe that they were doing for the Germans, through "tough love," what the Americans had done for themselves, laying the basis for a progressive, benevolently administered managerial democracy.[62]

When in October 1946, Senator Robert A. Taft complained in an address at Kenyon College that the Nuremberg Trials "violate that fundamental principle of American law that a man cannot be tried under an ex post facto statute" and that this practice by the victorious side showed "the spirit of vengeance," the distinguished

---

62. The educational and cultural division of the Office for Military Government in Germany treated its "reorientation" of the German people as being similar to "the work of Christian missionaries" and was concerned that it would continue after the Germans were left to govern themselves; see Gimbel, *American Occupation*, 251–52. By contrast, the head of the military government, Lucius D. Clay, only devotes about twenty-five pages of his memoirs, *Decision in Germany* (New York: Doubleday, 1950) to a (mostly perfunctory) treatment of reeducation. A long-overdue study of the Allied Occupation of Germany after the apparent reestablishment of German self-rule in September 1949 is Helmut Vogt's *Wächter der Bonner Republik: Die Alliierten Hohen Kommissare, 1949–1955* (Paderborn, Germany: Ferdinand Schöningh, 2004).

American leader faced numerous raging critics.[63] Beside the CIO, *New York Times,* the Democratic senate majority leader, and fifty acrimonious lawyers, prominent figures in his own party came out against Taft's insufficient devotion to antifascism. Taft expressed his legal and moral concerns about this precedent of trying one's enemies for "crimes against humanity" and for "conspiring against the peace," crimes that did not exist until the victors had devised them for use against the other side. He also made clear that the eleven Nazis who had been condemned to death were undoubtedly reprehensible; what he was protesting was trying them ex post facto and in some cases for misdeeds that the Soviets, who now sat in judgment over the Germans, had committed, together with their former Nazi allies.

That Taft reaped a bitter harvest for upholding what he believed to be Anglo-Saxon jurisprudence, tells volumes about the spirit in which Eisenhower's "crusade in Europe" had been carried out. If the Republican Party then and now consisted of mainline Protestants in the voting booth, Taft, a patrician, was shocked by the reaction of his fellow WASPs to a position of conscience that he thought they would applaud. Contrary to the observation of Carl Schmitt that in a constitutional republic "legality establishes legitimacy," what Taft learned was exactly the opposite. When New York Republican Thomas Dewey made the public statement "the Nazis had surely had a fair trial," what he was saying is that one did not have to worry about legal niceties, in view of the defendants' Nazi affiliations.[64]

Such attitudes were hardly confined to Communist sympathizers or to German émigrés but characterized a widely shared American attitude at the end of a righteous crusade. Thus observes a conservative nationalist critic of the Nazis, Ernst von Salomon (1902–1972), who, together with his Jewish wife, spent fifteen months in American captivity, from June 1945 through September 1946. Although Salomon tried to stay out of government entanglement throughout the Nazi period and was preoccupied with keeping

63. See James T. Patterson, *Mr. Republican: A Biography of Robert A. Taft* (Boston: Houghton and Mifflin, 1972), 326–28, 401–10.

64. Quoted in William J. Bosch, *Judgment in Nuremberg: Attitudes toward Major German War Crimes Trials* (Chapel Hill: University of North Carolina Press, 1970), 30.

his spouse hidden, the Americans threw them both into an intern-
ment camp, where, according to Salomon, they were subject to
beatings and other humiliations. Among the worst features of the
American occupation were the pseudo-scientific questionnaires
that the victors inflicted on him and his countrymen. As a "reactionary opponent" of the Nazis, Salomon was treated as miser-
ably as any concentration camp guard and forced to fill out inter-
minable forms devised by "trained professionals." In 1951, after
the American censorship had let up, Salomon produced his best-
seller *Der Fragebogen,* which dealt specifically with the role of
questionnaires in the reeducation of the Germans. He found this
impersonal meddling into people's lives a source of deep vexa-
tion—and one that helped turn him into a dogged enemy of American influence and of the American armed presence in Europe
during the Cold War.[65]

A Bavarian journalist (and Bavarian aristocrat from a prominent
"reactionary" anti-Nazi family), Caspar von Schrenck-Notzing,
produced an extensive study (now once again in print) in 1965
about the postwar reeducation undergone by his countrymen.
Schrenck-Notzing divides denazification, broadly understood, into
two phases. One was an immediate postwar stage characterized
by the Allied occupation, the application of censorship and intimi-
dation to achieve the desired social psychological effects, and the
promulgation of an official occupation view that stressed the cul-
pability of the German people for an evil history culminating in
Nazi atrocities. The later phase involved a more selective resump-
tion of the same charges, this time under German sponsorship.
What separated the two phases was the onset of the Cold War—
and the perceived American need to rehabilitate the Germans
into "democratic" allies against the Soviets.[66] What hastened this
alchemy, as understood by Schrenck-Notzing, was the resound-
ing victory of the Center-Right in the American congressional
elections of 1946 and the at least implicit repudiation of the pro-
Soviet policies pursued by the wartime Roosevelt administration.
In any case, by 1947 the United States was far less interested in

65. Ernst von Salomon, *Der Fragebogen,* new edition (Reinbek, Germany:
Rowohlt TB-Verlag, 2000); Carl Zuckmayer, *Deutschlandbericht* (Göttingen:
Wallstein Verlag, 2004).
66. Schrenck-Notzing, *Charakterwäsche,* 265–94.

prosecuting suspected Nazis and in applying Frankfurt School prescriptions to German family life than it was in fighting Communism at home and abroad.

What emerged in Germany, as the ideological counterpart of this American postwar anti-Communism, was what Schrenck-Notzing considers an intellectually fortified crusade against totalitarianism. This crusade was anchored in a prewar European liberal bourgeois outlook, and its representatives, who often came out of the academy, focused on the overlaps between Nazi and Communist practices. The chosen task of the antitotalitarians was the defense of a constitutional tradition that reflected Christian moral teachings and maintained spheres of individual and corporate authority that set limits on the central state. This liberal-conservative consensus prevailed among the defenders of the first postwar German chancellor, the patriarchal Catholic Rhinelander Konrad Adenauer (1876–1967). Among his entourage and the members of the German parliamentary Center-Right, one could find a certain range of anti-Communist, constitutionalist positions, from libertarian to regionalist and religious traditionalist. Significantly Adenauer, who might be described as a wartime reactionary anti-Nazi, went out of his way to subordinate German hopes for reunification to the shared goals of the Western alliance against the Soviets. Adenauer believed that standing beside the Americans in the struggle against Soviet Communism was more important than regaining German unity, if that had to be achieved by truckling to the Soviet masters of East Germany. Although Adenauer drew benefit from this Atlanticist position, for example, by integrating West Germany into NATO as a full-fledged and armed member, he also shunned Soviet overtures that might have alleviated if not totally removed the division between the two Germanies. It is hard to avoid the impression that the German leader truly believed that his Nazi and Soviet enemies were far more alike than different. And undoubtedly he was right in terms of their actions.[67]

From the fifties on, German legal and political theorists, with the Christian Democratic–Christian Social Union press at their

67. The definitive study of Adenauer and of his truly extraordinary impact on postwar German parliamentary politics is Frank Bösch, *Die Adenauer-CDU: Gründung, Aufstieg und Krise einer Erfolgspartei, 1945–1969* (Munich: Deutsche Verlags-Anstalt, 2001).

side, advanced the view of West Germany as a constitutional Christian society standing athwart the two related evils of twentieth-century Europe, Nazism and Communism. Into the eighties distinguished scholars, Joachim Ritter, Odo Marquard, Robert Spaemann, Hermann Lübbe, and Martin Kriele, continued to interpret the German Basic Law within the framework of this conservative-liberal tradition and confronted the eruption of New Left protest and violence with an elaborate defense of a constitutionally based ordered liberty.[68] What those who pursued this apologetic task did not consider was the adaptability of the Basic Law to radical ends. Protection of that law would eventually fall to those who were not notably devoted to a bourgeois civilization, a tendency that first became apparent in the 1950s in the province of Hesse, where "antifascist" social democrats took power and began to reinvestigate those in public life who had not been properly anti-Nazi, according to the canons of the radical Left.[69]

By the late fifties the momentum of the "antitotalitarian" Center-Right had been slowed down and even reversed. In contrast to what Habermas mocked as "an intellectually trivial phenomenon of reaction" caused by America's misunderstanding of Soviet intentions, a younger generation of German critics would stress the urgency of resuming the disrupted work of denazification. While the first phase targeted almost all of the German people, the second would begin by drawing distinctions between the good and bad kinds. It would address the problem of one's insufficiently repentant countrymen and the threatening presence of "nationalists" in German public life. Especially suspect were the connections between the parliamentary Center-Right and German refugees *(Vertriebene)* who had been driven out of Eastern Europe, usually with Soviet or Communist encouragement. To their critics, unless the opposite could be proved, these expellees

---

68. See Martin Kriele, *Einführung in die Staatslehre: Die geschichtliche Legitimitätsgrundlagen der demokratischen Verfassungsstaates,* 6th ed. (Stuttgart: Kohlhammer, 2003); Joachim Ritter, *Metaphysik und Politik: Studien zu Aristoteles und Hegel,* expanded edition with a postscript by Odo Marquard (Frankfurt am Main: Suhrkamp, 2003); and Robert Spaemann, *Zur Kritik der politischen Utopie: Zehn Kapitel politischer Philosophie* (Stuttgart: Cotta'sche Buchhandlung, 1977).

69. Schrenck-Notzing, *Charakterwäsche,* 274–75.

had been Nazi underlings and the fact that Adenauer and other "right-wing" German leaders refused to deal with Communist regimes that had authorized the expulsion of German minorities underscored their ties to the Nazi-nationalist past. By 1960, according to Schrenck-Notzing, one could discern in Germany a second surge of denazification that, unlike the first, would continue to gain ground.[70] The antinational mood that had been nurtured after the war had spread into the German population, and this happened after disappointed intellectuals had lamented the fact that the first reeducation had yielded to postwar economic recovery and patriotic feelings.

A radicalized German press, led by the newsmagazine *Spiegel,* pushed forward this new antinationalist orientation. It played up the embarrassments of German politicians on the right, such as minister of refugee affairs Theodor Oberländer, who was accused, for the most part wrongly, of having had Nazi associations; meanwhile journalists hastened to publicize classified military information in order to unsettle the anti-Communist establishment. The decision taken in 1962 by the German minister of defense (and an unabashed German patriot) Franz Josef Strauss to show his displeasure toward the *Spiegel,* for its leaking of classified materials, by impounding its press and by arresting several editors, backfired badly. It made the Christian Democratic government look authoritarian and seemed to confirm what the leftist opposition spoke of as its failure to break with Germany's undemocratic past.

The sixties also saw an attempt to overcome the German past by reconsidering the allegedly non-Nazi German past as a prelude to the Third Reich. Illustrating this Teutonophobic revisionism was the publication of Fritz Fischer's *Griff nach der Weltmacht* in 1964. A ponderous exposé of German ideological continuities from the Second Empire into the Nazi period, Fischer builds his argument on two cardinal points: Hitler's geopolitical aims in the East could be traced back to the government of William II and William's wartime chancellor Theobald von Bethmann-Hollweg (mistakenly viewed as a man of peace); and World War I was the work of German and Austrian expansionists who were active in public life and

70. Ibid., 279–88.

who deliberately fanned a conflagration throughout Europe. The responses to Fischer's thesis were ideologically predetermined: Spokesmen for the German Center and Center-Right, concentrated in the Union, emphatically refused to "accept German war guilt twice"; by contrast, the Fischerites, who gravitated toward the left wing of the SPD, presented Fischer's assignment of added German blame as essential for reassessing the nation's past.[71]

A persistent incriminatory style in this latter group leads from making the Germans solely responsible *(Alleinschuld)* for the Great War to an address delivered by German president Richard von Weizsäcker in May 1985, in which the entire nation was accused of complicity in the deportation of German Jews. From there, the road of fashionable self-recrimination can be seen winding on to the effusive reception bestowed by younger Germans in 1966 on Daniel Goldhagen, when this Jewish historian asserted that all Germans had readily collaborated in Hitler's anti-Semitic massacres. What confers on the German "cult of guilt" its permanent cast are its proponents and critics and their distinctive backgrounds. Despite the fact that Fischer as a young theologian rose through documented and often groveling collaboration with a Nazi-dominated university system, he was later transformed into the honored custodian of German conscience. Weizsäcker's father, Ernst, was a diplomat under the Third Reich who tried to keep the Vatican from protesting the deportation of Jews to concentration camps. The well-received statements by the younger Weizsäcker about collective, permanent German responsibility for Hitler's crimes may apply to the speaker far more than to most of his auditors. It might be said that the former president seized on a speaking opportunity to inflict on others the burdens of his family's unsavory past.[72]

71. In what might be a reductio ad absurdum of his own and the now prevalent German linkage thesis, Fischer's last book, *Hitler war kein Betriebsunfall* (Munich: C. H. Beck, 1998), had juxtaposed on the dust jacket the equally hysterical-looking faces of Kaiser Wilhelm and Hitler. The book does argue that there was no substantive ideological or political difference between Wilhelmine Germany and the Third Reich. See also Fritz Fischer, *Germany's War Aims in the First World War* (New York: Norton, 1967); and Fritz Fischer, *Wir sind nicht hineingeschlittert* (Hamburg: Rowohlt, 1983).

72. Nawratil, *Der Kult mit der Schuld*, 21–23; a provocative study of Fischer's career under the Third Reich is Hermann-Josef Grosse-Kracht, "Fritz Fischer

Moreover, among Fischer's most hated critics was the distinguished historian Gerhard Ritter, who barely escaped the war with his life. Ritter had actively supported the participants in the doomed 1944 plot against Hitler; nonetheless, he was subject to a hypocritical charge hurled by Fischerites that as a reactionary nationalist the Allies should have removed him from academic life. Ritter's remarks about Fischer's research and conclusions are unfailingly professional judgments; moreover, his study of Imperial Germany and the war is at least as critical of German statecraft as it is of the Central Powers' encirclement by the other side. All of Fischer's major German critics, including Golo Mann, Egmont Zechlin, Karl-Dietrich Erdmann, and Ritter, stood squarely within the postwar liberal constitutional consensus and, as far as this author can ascertain, were in exile or, unlike Fischer, whom the Americans jailed as a Nazi propagandist, avoided association with the Third Reich. Not one of these historians glorified the German leaders of 1914 or tried to cover up German diplomatic ineptitude that contributed to the eruption of the war. What they were presumed to be guilty of was Habermas's charge against Nolte, ignoring the task of national repentance that began with the postwar reeducation of the Germans.[73]

At the same time, it is foolish to brand as Communist the mainstream attempts at jump-starting this once stalled reeducation.

---

und der deutsche Protestantismus," *Zeitschrift für Neuere Theologie-Geschichte* 10, no. 2 (2003), 196–223.

73. For criticism of the Fischer thesis, see the study of Germany's 1914 chancellor, Theobald von Bethmann-Hollweg, by Hans Jarausch, *The Enigmatic Chancellor* (Princeton: Princeton University Press, 1972); John Langdon, *July 1914: The Long Debate, 1918–1990* (New York: Berg, 1991), 109–29; Karl-Dietrich Erdmann, "Zur Beurteilung Bethmann-Hollweg," in *Geschichte in Wissenschaft und Unterricht* 15 (1964), 525–40; Paul Gottfried, "History or Hysteria," *Alternative* 8, no. 4 (July 1975), 16–18; and Niall Ferguson, *The Pity of War* (London: Penguin, 1998), 106–8. The tendency among Fischerites in their emphasis on Imperial German war guilt to ignore the other side's reckless conduct in July 1914 raises unavoidable methodological questions. For the British cabinet's, particularly Churchill's, anything but irenic response to the continental situation after the assassination of the Austrian archduke on June 28, see John Charmley, *Churchill: The End of Glory* (London: Harcourt, Brace, 1993), 95–115; M. Brock's "Britain Enters the War," in R. J. W. Evans and H. Pogge von Strandmann, *The Coming of the First World War* (Oxford: Oxford University Press, 1998), 145–78; and Hunt Tooley's *The Western Front* (Hampshire, England: Palgrave-Macmillan, 2003), 1–40.

There is nothing even vaguely Marxist, let alone Marxist-Leninist, about the "overcoming of the past" journalism and historical narratives that were emerging in Germany by the sixties. Although Fischer and his acolytes do not hesitate to go after German commercial and industrial leaders for abetting the arms race and imperial expansion, they also do not exempt either German labor leaders or German unions from their censures. The German working class and its advocates were supposedly as nationalistic and expansionist as other Germans, having been afflicted by what is seen as a peculiarly Teutonic chauvinism. Viewed in isolation, such a judgment may not seem entirely unreasonable. Unfortunately it fails to take into account the nationalisms raging among Germany's neighbors or those actions by rival powers that might shed light on German imperial conduct in international situations. But what Fischer definitely does not do is replicate a standard Marxist understanding of the First World War as a struggle among competing capitalist countries that eventually spilled over into a general conflict. Rather, he is stressing the disastrous consequences of Germany's unique nationalist illusions that he argues caused a (for Germany) desired European war in 1914—and by implication fed into later Nazi ideology. While it might have benefited the Soviets during the Cold War to get the Germans to obsess over the real and imaginary evils of their history, the Fischerites were neither theoretical Marxists nor economic determinists. They were pushing Nazi attitudes back into an earlier age and discrediting the generation of their grandparents as well as that of their "Nazi" parents.

But such an enterprise did not appeal outside of Germany to leftists exclusively. The German Teutonophobia that took off in the sixties, and which in Germany led toward Habermas and the Post-Marxist Left, resonated well among British Tories and American neoconservatives. Paul Johnson, Donald Kagan, Liah Greenfeld, and other historians who cannot possibly be identified with any establishment Left have vigorously defended the Fischerite interpretation of the German Empire and of World War I.[74] German Teutonophobes, who dwell on the evils of their country's pre-

---

74. See Paul Johnson's *Modern Times: The World from the Twenties to the Eighties* (New York: Harper and Row, 1983), particularly 106–8. On the basis of what

Nazi past, enjoy the endorsement of those who view the
mans as their preferred historic enemy. Nothing connects th.. ...
tinational position in Germany or elsewhere to any Marxist tradition or even to postwar German Social Democracy, which did
not feature anti-German sentiment any more than its center-right
opposition.[75]

It might be allowed to mention here my own experience, as a
young critic of the Fischer thesis, who subsequently incurred the
anger of the new American conservatives (neoconservatives). This
group of engaged Teutonophobes and moderate critics of the American welfare state harassed me professionally for decades: because
I am a descendant of Austrian Jewish refugees from the Nazis,
they thought I should continue to be angry at the Germans for
what had happened under the Third Reich. But my task in this
case was not to defend the Nazis—as opposed to underlining the
shared blame of all the belligerents for the First World War.
Opposition to the once settled view on the subject had arisen not
so much from new documentary evidence as it did from resur-
gent Teutonophobia.

But the continued success of the Fischer thesis points to a
development that goes beyond the Germans or any selective anxiety about genocide, which noticeably excludes the mass murders
committed by the Left. It reflects to some degree the weakening
of what remains of a bourgeois society on both sides of the Atlantic.
And this trend can be traced to the general withering of Euro-
American national allegiances and to the rejection of traditional
cultural identities in favor of global and multicultural values. Such

---

seems far from clinching proof, the Tory Atlanticist Johnson finds the "case for
German war guilt [in 1914] to be established beyond doubt" (106). In *On the
Origin of War and the Preservation of Peace* (New York: Doubleday, 1995), especially 169–73, Donald Kagan, a neoconservative advocate and historian of the
Peloponnesian War, likewise introduces Fischer's thesis as self-evident but fails
to consider the accumulated counterarguments. See also the pervasively Teutonophobic study done by Liah Greenfeld, *Nationalism: Five Roads to Modernity*
(Cambridge: Harvard University Press, 1992). A fitting subject for a book is the
unremitting Teutonophobia that continues to rage among Anglo-American
political intellectuals. What began as a leftist fixation has moved, under neoconservative guidance, steadily rightward.

75. On the break of the Fischerites from the patriotic Left, see Harmut
Pogge von Strandsmann, "Warum die Deutschen den Krieg wollten," in *Die
Zeit*, March 11, 1988, 19.

a process affected the Germans more profoundly than it did the Americans, in view of the relentlessly revisited burdens of their history. This "overcoming of the German past," while only a sub-genus of the demands placed on all Western Christian societies to divest themselves of their pre-postmodern legacies, has had expanding psychological effects. One can easily find these effects in the German allergy to military engagements, particularly against Third World adversaries, and in the conspicuous eagerness of Chancellor Gerhard Schröder to join in the celebration of the D-Day landing, which had resulted in the deaths of tens of thousands of German soldiers.[76] It is not unreasonable to link Germany's present self-contempt and the receptiveness of its declining population to Post-Marxist trends to what the postwar occupation helped establish. Just as Jacob Burckhardt proclaimed the Italian Renaissance to be the "first-born son of modern Europe," so too did postwar Germany after some hesitation bring forth with American midwifery a Post-Marxist leftist society. To the present generation of Germans has been vouchsafed the fateful experiment of living in and promoting such a reality.

76. See the summary of Schröder's presentation at the D-Day ceremonies in the *New York Times,* June 7, 2004, 10.

5

THE POST-MARXIST LEFT
AS POLITICAL RELIGION

■ Soft Despotism

Studies about Eric Voegelin's seminal investigation of the ties between politics and cosmology, *The Political Religions* (1938), might by now fill up several capacious library shelves. But what is intended here is not to break new interpretive ground but to apply a fruitful concept to research in progress. The Post-Marxist Left represents (with certain qualifications made in the first chapter) a distinctive political religion. It should therefore be understood as a would-be successor to a traditional belief system, one parasitic on Judeo-Christian symbols but equipped with its own transformational myths and end-of-history vision. To whatever extent this Left also reveals traces of a "Gnostic" myth, it may be necessary to ascertain its origin in an ancient Near Eastern civilization. Voegelin and the German-Jewish scholar Jakob Taubes have both focused critical attention on the relation between ancient Christian heresies and modern political cultures.[1]

This chapter will explore such parallels but only where appropriate. The main focus is the correspondence between redemptive religion and a particular contemporary project, aimed at changing human nature in preparation for a perfected History. A qualification

1. Eric Voegelin, *Die politischen Religionen* (Vienna: Springer Verlag, 1938); Eric Voegelin, *The New Science of Politics* (Chicago: University of Chicago Press, 1952); Jakob Taubes, *Gnosis und Politik* (Munich: Ferdinand Schöning/Fink Verlag, 1984), 230–48.

stated in the first chapter should be repeated here. Voegelin and Taubes developed their models of political religion with an eye toward the hard tyrannies of Nazi Germany and Stalin's Russia. But what is being surveyed in this chapter is a less obtrusive form of oppression, one closer to what Tocqueville called *le doux despotisme*. It is political management that eventually approaches total control but with less and less need for physical force. In this respect as well as in its faceless leadership, it is different from the totalitarian behemoths of the thirties and forties, which gave rise to what German historian Ernst Nolte has characterized as the "European civil war."[2] While Nolte's interpretation of this war is open to challenge, he is correct about its effects on European political life. The traumatic clashes engaged in by the brutal political religions of the past continue to cast their shadow.

■ A Lingering Communist Deity

The appeal of a Communist god remains a critical point of reference for explaining the current European parliamentary Left. Illustrations from earlier chapters might serve to demonstrate this fact. French and Italian Socialist-Communist coalitions complain perpetually about "fascist residues" but demand at the same time collective amnesia about the murderous history of Marxist-Leninism. Moreover, the Socialist and Communist presses in France greeted Solzhenitsyn's work on the Soviet labor camps in the 1970s as a hysterically anti-Communist tirade. The French translation of his *Gulag Archipelago* brought forth attacks from across the journalistic Left, including in the Socialist *L'Unité*, about Sozhenitsyn's alleged attempts to divert attention from American imperialism in Latin America, his outrageous comparisons of Communism and fascism, and his incitement of the Cold War, for which the Americans were held responsible.[3] In 1997, French premier Lionel Jospin, in response to an interpellation from opposi-

2. Alexis de Tocqueville, *De la démocratie en Amérique* (Paris: Flammarion, 1981), 2:19, 385–88; Nolte, *Der europäische Bürgerkrieg;* Ernst Nolte, *Lehrstücke oder Tragödie: Beiträge zur Interpretation der Geschichte* (Cologne: Böhlau Verlag, 1993).

3. See Sévillia, *Le terrorisme*, 99–121; and André Glucksman, *La cuisinière et le mangeur d'hommes* (Paris: Seuil, 1975).

tion parties in the French assembly, refused to acknowledge Soviet atrocities under Stalin and praised the Communists in general as his brave fellow-warriors in their shared crusade against fascism.[4]

The issue at that time was the recently published *Black Book of Communism*, by Stéphane Courtois, which detailed the extent of Communist mass murder since the Russian Revolution. Jospin gave the impression of being utterly indifferent to one totalitarian holocaust, after having cosponsored legislation in 1990 that made it a criminal offense to deny the received account of Nazi crimes. Jospin may have been following the Paris intelligentsia grouped around *Le Monde*, which flew into a rage when Stéphane Courtois brought out the *Black Book* and asserted that Communists in the twentieth century had killed as many as 100 million victims, which put the magnitude of their brutality well beyond that of Hitler and his followers. To compare Communist misdeeds to those of the Nazis, complained Jean-Louis Margolin in *Le Monde*, is to deny that "Communism seeks to liberate mankind while Nazism is a racist doctrine that relegates most of humanity to the shadows." Or as another Paris journalist, Roland Leroy, put it, "at the heart of Communism is love of humanity; at the heart of Nazism is hatred of the human race."[5]

Likewise in Germany, prominent Social Democrats, and various literati, including Gunter Grass and Jürgen Habermas, worked overtime in the eighties defending the East German Communist regime. Whether a condign punishment for Germans because of the taint *(Erblast)* of their past conduct or a worthy experiment in socialist humanism, the German government to the east became for the West German Left an object of infatuation. Social Democratic provincial administrations jammed airwaves that transmitted East German protests, including those of East German social democrats; in 1991 the self-appointed voices of German conscience opposed the unification of the East Germans with a West German "capitalist" society. Somehow the East Germans were imagined to have broken decisively from the German "authoritarian" past by virtue of calling themselves Marxist-Leninists and by referring

4. *Le Monde*, November 14, 1997, 8.
5. Ibid., October 31, 1997, 8; Roland Leroy, "Bouillon de culture," *Le Journal du Dimanche*, November 2, 1997, 1–2.

to their enemies as "fascists." More remarkable still is the view, commonly held among German intellectuals, that their heavily taxed and painfully regulated economy testifies to the evils of a non-socialist free market. And in a country where federal and provincial censorship and government investigators *(Verfassungsschutzmänner)* operate against the makers of "extremist" statements, which are almost always interpreted as those coming from the right, intellectuals and journalists nonetheless believe that fascism is on the loose. It was the East Germans, because of the ascribed grace of Communist affiliation, whose government had supposedly worked harder to "overcome the past" *(Vergangenheitsbewältigung)*.[6]

■ A Post-Marxist Age

These observations do not prove, and are not intended to prove, that the current European Left is still Marxist. To restate the argument of the first chapter: Except for certain by now instinctive quirks, such as defending Communist dictatorships as humanitarian learning experiences, decrying those who call attention to Communist atrocities, and describing one's opposition as "fascist" and being in need of resocialization, the European Left has become Post-Marxist. It is socialist only residually and does not generally favor the nationalization of productive forces or the confiscation of wealth. What makes the European Left what it is today is at least partly its justification for a quasi-market economy. According to French Socialist and architect of the EU, Jacques Delors, and longtime Italian Communist functionary and founder of the post-Communist party of the Italian Left, Giorgio Napolitano, a market economy is today both desirable and inescapable for Europeans. It has opened the door to material prosperity while helping to destroy divisive national identities. Commerce and international trade have moved European societies into a postnational phase and helped liberate women and minorities from the restric-

---

6. These concerns about residual fascism in the two societies under discussion are noted in Günter Müchter's "Die moralische Abrüstung der Linken und die Erblast DDR," in *Medien Dialog* 8, no. 98: 23–25; see also Gottfried, *Multiculturalism*, 17–38; and Habermas, *Die Moderne*, 75–86.

tions of an older, bourgeois world.[7] Rather than being a pillar of this archaic world, a now tamed capitalism has become the hand-maiden of multiculturalism.

Hans-Olaf Henkel, president of the Federal Union of German Industrialists and professor of industrial sciences at the University of Mannheim, has made the same argument with equal force. According to Henkel, in his book *Die Macht der Freiheit*, international commerce has accelerated two positive trends: the movement of populations across national borders and an increasingly pluralistic culture within European societies. Both are viewed as signs of the "power of freedom," to which Henkel claims to have devoted his life as an advocate of corporate growth, as an IBM executive, and finally, as an academic.[8] This position has brought discomfort to French leftist communitarian Pierre-André Taguieff, who recently published a polemic against the dangers of *bougisme*, allowing human relations to be determined by economic transactions and multinational corporations.[9] But Taguieff does not offer an alternative system of production; nor does he call for a return to traditional national or ethnic identities, which as a French Jew of the Left in what had been a Christian Europe he may find personally threatening. In any case it is hard to see any significant degree of economic Marxist-Leninism in the recently published, mostly European works directed against corporate capitalist globalism. Whether one looks at Antonio Negri and Emmanuel Todd telling us that American economic imperialism is drawing to a close, Jürgen Habermas bewailing the fact that Euro-American capitalists have distorted democratic communication, or Taguieff

7. See Jacques Delors's remarks in *Le Monde*, October 4, 2003, 8; and Napolitano, *Europa, America dopo l'89*. For an essay that obscures this point of general economic convergence and exaggerates the prevalence of economic radicalism on the current European Left, see "La droite cherche à séduire les milieux intellectuels," in *Le monde: Les dossiers et documents* (April 2004), 2.

8. Hans-Olaf Henkel, *Die Macht der Freiheit* (Schaffhausen: Econ-Ullstein, 2002); see also Lorenz Jäger, epilogue to Hans-Hermann Hoppe, *Demokratie: Der Gott, der keiner war* (Leipzig: Manuscriptum Verlagsbuchhandlung, 2003), 541–47. Jäger and Hoppe make sarcastic comments about Henkel's "democratic globalist" vision but do so without rejecting a market economy.

9. Pierre-André Taguieff, *Résister au bougisme: Démocratie forte contre la mondialisation techno-marchande* (Paris: Mille et une nuits, 2001), 75–77; see also Pierre-André Taguieff, *L'effacement de l'avenir* (Paris: Galilée, 2000), 33–37.

appealing to the ideal of self-generating socialist communities, missing are the customary Marxist grand schemes for structural change. No longer do we encounter nonnegotiable demands for public ownership of production or the expropriation of the capitalist class. By now the disintegration of a distinctive laboring class in France and in Italy and the erosion of a predominantly working-class Communist electorate in those countries have worked their effect on the European Left.

The reason for this changed Left is not primarily the one proposed by University of Turin professor of history Bruno Bongiovanni in *La caduta dei communismi,* who explained that the fall of the Soviet empire initiated a chain reaction leading to the disintegration of Communist parties and Communist ideology across Europe.[10] In the *quindicennio* that Bongiovanni examines, from the fall of Saigon to Ho Chi Minh's armies in 1975 to the breakdown of the Eastern European Communist system by 1990, multiple social changes had occurred in Western and Central Europe that would bring about the Left's irreversible transformation. Electoral power would flow from the Communists to the Socialists in France and in Italy, and the old-fashioned economic Marxism with loyalty to the Soviets would be replaced by lifestyle radicalism and ultimately multiculturalism. The term "cultural Marxism" used to describe this process has only limited value. It makes the transformation underway identical with the Frankfurt School or with the way Theodor Adorno, Herbert Marcuse, and others of their persuasion viewed their cultural mission. But calling for anti-bourgeois family arrangements or unrestricted sexual expressiveness has little or nothing to do with dialectical materialism or with the economic restructuring of bourgeois society.[11] Even more problematic for applying Marxist labels to the current Left is this Left's loss of interest in socialist economic planning. While the Post-Marxist Left certainly favors progressive income taxes, extensive

10. Bruno Bongiovanni, *La caduta dei comunismi* (Milan: Garzanti Editore, 1995), 1–39.

11. A critical understanding of Georg Lukacs and the Frankfurt School characterized Lucio Colletti, while this later supporter of the center-right Casa Libertà still referred to himself as a *marxista irreducibile.* See his two-volume anthology, *Il Marxismo e Hegel;* and Gottfried, "Marx contra Hegel."

welfare states, and government-run educational systems, in none of these stands does it differ sharply from the center-right parties in the United States or in Europe.

In fact this leftist economic-social vision overlaps not only that of the Federal Union of German Industrialists, and its president, but also that of the world as conceived by American neoconservatives. The promise of the present age for the European Left is more or less the vision articulated by Francis Fukuyama in his famous "End of History" essay published in the *National Interest*. "Liberal democracy," as the breakdown of national borders and national consciousness, governments responsive to the people, international commerce, and human rights, Fukuyama proclaims, is the wave of the future, after the last antidemocratic ideology of the twentieth century had made and lost its bid for world domination.[12] Although not committed to the welfare-state anti-Communism of the American neoconservatives and less than enthusiastic about their scheme for an American imperial mission to spread "democratic values," the European Left does accept the same core vision, a modified form of capitalism as the icebreaker for a new global society, including the empowerment of women, support for generous immigration policies, and the movement toward transnational political identities. When American neoconservative journalist Ben Wattenberg explains repeatedly that his "American nationalism" consists of wanting to bring human rights and secular democracy to the entire world, the European Left should find little to quibble about, except for the application of American power to achieve Wattenberg's goal. A more homogenized humanity moving across open borders would be equally acceptable to both American neoconservatives and most European leftist intellectuals, however much they may disagree about the United States' present Middle Eastern politics.[13]

Prominent American neoconservative journalist and author Stephen Schwartz has argued in the *National Review* that those who are fighting for global democracy should view Leon Trotsky

12. See Fukuyama, "End of History?" 3–6; and Fukuyama, *End of History and the Last Man*.

13. Ben J. Wattenberg, "Even the Left Can Learn," syndicated in the *New York Post*, April 30, 1999, 37; Wattenberg, *First Universal Nation*.

as a worthy forerunner. In the struggle against "fascist" Islamicists who engage in terror and express anti-Jewish sentiments, the anti-Stalinist internationalist Trotsky is someone whom Schwartz believes that his side should venerate. No wonder an English critic of American imperialism, John Laughland, mocks this "Marxism without Stalin" haunting the American establishment Right. A bit of "welfare state capitalism," maintains Laughland, is a small enough price to be paid by those trying to create a denationalized world order. Swedish political theorist Claes G. Ryn replicates Laughland's animadversions when he remarks in *America the Virtuous:* "Of those in the West today who are passionate advocates of capitalism and want it introduced all over the world, many are former Marxists. The shift from being a Marxist to becoming a missionary for capitalism may be less drastic than is commonly assumed." Furthermore, Ryn asserts with reference to American neoconservatives: "A person may advocate capitalism not so much because he utterly rejects Marx's vision of a new society as because he regards the revolution of the proletariat and the socialist organization of production as blind alleys for realizing an essentially egalitarian society—A person may endorse capitalism because letting the market do its work is the best way to uproot backward beliefs and related sociopolitical structures."[14]

■ The Second Reality

Despite the overlaps between the two, what distinguishes the European Left from American empire boosters are two intertwined features, the intensity of friend-enemy distinctions and the invocation of what Voegelin, adapting the concept of Austrian novelist Heimito von Doderer (1896–1966), calls the "second reality." The second feature, which is taken from von Doderer, a "worldview" marked by *Apperzeptionsverweigerung,* "a systematic refusal to apperceive reality" because of a quest for transcendence

14. Stephen Schwartz, "Trotskycons?" in *National Review Online,* July 11, 2003, www.nationalreview.com; John Laughland, "An Invisible Government," January 26, 2004, www.sandersresearch.com/Sanders/NewsManager/ShowNewsGen .aspx; Claes G. Ryn, *America the Virtuous: The Crisis of Democracy and the Quest for Empire* (New Brunswick, N.J.: Transaction Publishers, 2003), 148.

through "political conviction," shapes the first feature.[15] What Voegelin considers symptomatic of the "second reality," looking at things "through a kind of slit in an armored car through which one grasps only arbitrary facets of reality," causes one to exaggerate the malevolence of anyone suspected of holding ideologically incompatible opinions. Those who reject one's program for human betterment are less than respectful opposition. They are to the Post-Marxist Left "right-wing extremists" and "fascists," or at the very least *fascisants*, who have forgotten the lessons of Auschwitz and who plan to treat Third World minorities, homosexuals, and the transgendered the way Hitler did European Jewry.

While the Marxist agenda of the European Left has changed, what has not is the ill will vented on those who resist its interests. Whether fighting to allow unrestricted Third World immigration into Europe, gay marriage, the lowering of the legal age for male homosexual prostitution, the building of mosques at the expenses of European taxpayers, this Left is implacably hostile to those who think differently and trace this deviation to fascist sympathies. Critics of this stylistic trend, such as Alain Finkielkraut and Jean Sévillia, have noted the "biological revulsion," approaching Hitler's descriptions of the Jews, that now marks French journalism. The journalistic and literary Left routinely applies such pseudo-biological, visceral terminology to those who depart from its pre-scribed point of view. According to Finkielkraut, whose family were Nazi refugees, it is impossible to peruse the French publications *Le Monde* and *Libération* without recalling the rhetorical excesses of the Third Reich. An antifascist "Manichean vision," he observes in *Le Figaro-Magazine,* "leads to a simplistic moral dualism instead of a political understanding of the world." What has taken the place of analysis is a "medical biological vocabulary of eradication."[16]

Equally noticeable is the return to an imprecatory style charac-teristic of the post–World War II Communist press. Thus when the Soviet defector Victor Kravchenko published in 1946 *I Chose*

---

15. See Eric Voegelin, *Hitler and the Germans,* trans. and ed. Detlev Clemens and Brendon Purcell (Columbia: University of Missouri Press, 1999), 255; and Heimito von Doderer, *Die Merowinger und die totale Familie* (Munich: Deutscher Taschenbuch Verlag, 1981).

16. *Le Figaro-Magazine,* April 10, 1998, 18.

Freedom, an autobiography that dwells on the savagery of Stalin's rule, not only the French Communist *L'Humanité* but the more generically leftist *Lettres Françaises* denounced Kravchenko, without evidence, as a Nazi agent. The same defamation was directed even more implausibly against Margarete Buber-Neumann, daughter of Jewish theologian Martin Buber, who had miraculously survived Soviet and Nazi labor camps during the war. After fleeing Germany with her Communist husband and going to Soviet Russia, the Neumanns were almost immediately arrested by the Soviet secret police. Frau Neumann was first sent to Siberia but then returned to Germany and interned at Ravensbruck, following the Soviet-Nazi pact in 1939. She published a controversial memoir, which came out in French in 1949, about her wartime experiences, which deeply offended French Communists and French Communist fellow travelers. Her unkind references to Soviet labor camps, which were supposedly educational institutions, suggested to the Communist faithful that the memoirist was serving as a Nazi propagandist.[17]

But by the seventies such surreal charges gave way on the European left to the protest that critics of the Communists were aggravating the Cold War. Mentioning Soviet imperfections at this point would only lead to greater American belligerence in prosecuting that struggle; this in turn would force the Warsaw Pact governments to arm themselves more heavily in reaction to Western saber rattling. Anti-Communists were also guilty of moral asymmetry, a charge that Delors leveled at Jean-François Revel, the former Communist author of *La tentation totalitaire* (1976), who had focused on Communist crimes while making light of American colonialism. One should not be overly severe, says Delors, in describing the Communists' difficulties in building a socialist society out of poverty, particularly when their critics have been indulgent of an expansive capitalist power allied to right-wing militarists.[18]

After the fall of the Soviet empire, the signals on the European left changed to what they had been in the late forties. Such a development took place, however, without Soviet power or Soviet

17. Sévillia, *Le terrorisme,* 24–33; John Margoline, *La condition inhumaine* (Paris: Calmann-Lévy, 1949); Alain Besançon, *Une génération* (Paris: Juillard, 1987).

18. Jacques Delors, *Le Monde,* January 16, 1976, 8.

interests playing a critical role. It also occurred among Socialists more dramatically than among Communists, that is, within parties that in the fifties and sixties were far from friendly to the Soviets. Alain Besançon and François Furet both observe that a deliberate "amnesia about Communism" and its crimes led the European Left into returning to antifascist demonology as a cover-up for their historical embarrassments.[19] In the nineties, Paris newspapers and feuilletons were likely to stress Nazi crimes together with real or imaginary French collaborators, while taking pains not to mention those whom the Communists had killed or imprisoned. Pro-Communist amnesia about the gulags, according to Besançon, has fueled a journalistic and political fixation on Auschwitz that goes on and on. Exemplifying this obsession was a tiff in the Italian House of Deputies in April 2000 between the Center-Left (which now includes the Communists) and the Center-Right concerning a day of remembrance for Italian victims of the Holocaust. When the Left proposed such a solemn holiday, partly to rivet attention on the presumed crimes of the Italian nationalist Right in supporting fascist anti-Semitism, the opposition countered that it would support the concept if the day of remembrance was expanded to commemorate "all victims of totalitarianism." The Italian Left and its press then expressed its displeasure that the present governing coalition would not "come to terms with its own past" and persisted in raising the inflammatory issue of Communist crimes committed somewhere else.[20]

But the crimes were not irrelevant, since the Italian Communist Party doggedly defended the Soviet position throughout the postwar years, including the Soviet invasion of Hungary in 1956 and the military occupation of Czechoslovakia in 1968. Following the retreat of the German army, the Italian Communists, together with other leftist partisans, the Azionisti, were involved in the slaughter of tens of thousands of their countrymen, as fascist or German collaborators, a situation that allowed the Communists to wreak indiscriminate revenge on their political opponents.[21] It

19. François Furet and Ernst Nolte, *Fascisme et communisme* (Paris: Plon, 1998); Alain Besançon, *Le malheur du siècle* (Paris; Fayard, 1998).

20. *Il Mattino*, April 17, 2000.

21. Silvio Bertoldi, "Roma liberata: Giustizia alla italiana," *Corriere della Sera*, November 25, 1996, 19.

is furthermore impossible to see what connection there is between the present Italian Center-Right and the Nazi puppet state that deported Italian Jewry to concentration camps in 1944. Perhaps the connection we are supposed to infer is that those who are tactless enough to notice Communist massacres might also favor Hitler's Final Solution.

■ Good versus Evil

Having pointed out the link between the rhetorical obsession with fascist dangers and a suppression of any memory about leftist or Stalinist crimes, it might be appropriate to turn to another, less-obvious reason for the current antifascism. This posture, according to Furet, provides "the essential criterion for allowing us to distinguish the Good and the Evil." It therefore makes no difference, for the European Left, whether the Nazis and Communists were behaviorally more alike than different. Those who supported the Communists should be praised for exhibiting "good intentions," while those who opposed them, we are made to think, would have applauded Hitler's genocide. The Left is about purity of intention, which must be demonstrated through ceaseless combat against the impure. Moreover, since ideological impurity, as understood by European intellectuals of the Left (who are cited at length in my book *Multiculturalism and the Politics of Guilt*), is always "lurking" or offering those who are vulnerable "tempting foods," it is imperative to remain vigilant in the face of this peril.[22]

This attempt by the "just" to ban "undemocratic dispositions" has taken perhaps an extreme institutional form in Germany, where the federal and provincial courts and agencies claiming to be protecting the German Constitution have dealt harshly with inadmissible thought. What has happened, as noted by Christian Graf von Krockow, Hans-Gerd Jaschke, and other German commentators who cannot conceivably be associated with the Right, is that "hostility to the Constitution" *(Verfassungsfeindlichkeit)* has

---

22. Gottfried, *Multiculturalism*, 88–100; Bernard-Henri Lévy, *L'idéologie française* (Paris: Grasset, 1981), 263.

been interpreted to mean "betraying a disposition" that clashes with a politically correct democracy.[23] While the West German Basic Law in 1949 provided for judicial intervention against party formations seen as a threat to the constitutional order, a provision demanded by the American occupiers of postwar Germany, more recently this option has been used to reconstruct German society. What have been declared illegal are ideas that impede an ongoing "revolution to catch up" *(eine nachholende Revolution)*. The German Left is carrying out a new founding of the Federal Republic, on the grounds that the bourgeois democracy created in 1949 did not go far enough to break with the Nazi past. German courts and the appointed protectors of German democracy, viewed as "a teleological structure of meaning," have worked to marginalize ideological and emotional nonconformists. True democratic practice, they contend, requires the operation of *their* values and sentiments and the outlawing of those competitors for public office and state-controlled academic posts who are known to hold "undemocratic" views.[24]

In Germany this campaign has also been waged against symbols and sounds that are thought to threaten the bureaucratically shaped pluralism that gives "moral content" to German democracy. Besides Nazi paraphernalia, monarchist, pagan, or overly exotic symbols have been subject to federal and provincial bans. This winter German police arrested people who were singing the "Deutschland Lied," since the words of the German anthem were considered to convey nationalist and possibly fascist sentiments. A recent spoof on the TV series *South Park* in which the protagonists

23. Hans-Gerd Jaschke, *Streitbare Demokratie und inner Sicherheit* (Westdeutscher Verlag: Opladen, 1991), 66–82; Christian Graf von Krockow, "30 Jahre streitbare Demokratie: Zum Problem des Wertewandels," *Gegenwartskunde Sonderheft* (1979), 5–12.

24. See Claus Nordbruch, *Der Verfassungsschutz: Organisation-Spitzel-Skandale* (Tübingen: Hohenrain, 1991). Nordbruch's comprehensive exposé of government surveillance in Germany, for unmasking "dangers to the constitutional order," and of the crass partisan uses to which this "disposition snooping" *(Gesinnungsschnüffelei)* has been put, does not seem to warrant the observation that this surveillance could be made to work if directed against real threats to the German government. Not surprisingly, the object of his study proceeded to "unmask" Nordbruch as an "extremist" after he had reported on its activities.

were sent to a German concentration camp designed to enforce multiculturalism may be prophetic. One cannot think of a country in which "political religion" has done so well since its first "catch-up revolution" of the 1930s.

If this bid for thought control divides the Western world into the reprobate and the "light-bearers" or "cleansed ones," there are in this Gnostic mythology the in-between types who remain targets of persuasion. Those waiting to be saved are neither the fascist reprobates nor on the level of those already saved, the *phosphoroi* and *katharismenoi*. They are linked to a world in which there is still what Jürgen Habermas calls a "democracy deficit." It is a world that requires the ministrations of those who have been lifted into light and who are trying to carry their revelation to others. For example, defective democrats cannot really engage in conversation with those who think differently; they need conversation-masters to set up the rules for their verbal exchanges. Social Democratic jurist Volker Hauff asserts that his countrymen suffer from "a lack of democratic substance" because the "still unconquered vestiges [of the undemocratic past] continue to operate in our history in subterranean fashion, while the continuities of German history are still surreptitiously present." Given this situation, it would appear irresponsible to leave communications and politics in bourgeois hands, in which they would be subject to undemocratic or fascist defilement.[25]

The persistence of defiling continuities in the European subconscious, which make it resistant to a multicultural identity, further require the banning of ideas and art that refer back, however distantly, to the fascist pollutant. Thus it is not enough for progressive Europeans to punish those found guilty of *Nazi* "Holocaust denial" or those who distribute their works. It is equally important to go after those who are allegedly distracting attention from this problem by making a fuss over Soviet victims or by lamenting the Allied bombing during World War II inflicted on German and other Central European civilians. Both the French national press and German *Verfassungsschutzmänner* (officials charged with inves-

25. Volker Hauff, *Sprachlose Politik* (Frankfurt am Main: Fischer Verlag, 1979), 25.

tigating "extremist" threats to German democracy) have treated such attitudes as being related to explicit acts of Holocaust denial, and European governments energetically keep files on those who diffuse them.

On February 28, 2004, the exhibit "The Right through and from the Middle" was opened in Cologne in what had once been a Gestapo headquarters. This widely publicized exhibit was designed to make viewers aware of past and present German "right-wing extremism." Nazi leaders are shown among the right-wing extremists, but the exhibit, organized by German "antifascists" and funded by major political parties, also depicted the Christian Democratic–Christian Social Union as inciters of fascism.[26] The reason was the more stringent requirements that the Union tried to impose in 2003 on "asylum seekers" asking to settle in Germany. Whatever the merits of that position for alleged asylum seekers, it is hard to grasp how it is related to the actions of the Gestapo at the same site sixty years earlier.

Another manifestation of "fascist" evil, one offering a stumbling block for the weak, was discovered when *Le Monde* dissuaded the French government in 2000 from reburying the remains of composer Hector Berlioz in the Panthéon. Despite his contributions to romantic music and his composition of one of the most brilliant nineteenth-century symphonies, the reinterment of Berlioz in the company of other French creative geniuses, according to *Le Monde,* would be "striking a false note."[27] His work supposedly raises questions about Berlioz's commitment to republican values (Berlioz was a monarchist) and to diversity. The French and German press had demanded during the preceding summer that the Salzburg *Sommerfestspiel* cancel a performance of his opera *Les Troyens,* which celebrates Roman antiquities as portrayed in Virgil's epic, *The Aeneid.* This controversial artistic production would have supposedly given aid and comfort to Latin fascists, a possibility that

26. *Junge Freiheit,* April 9, 2004, 20; see also the website of the organizing antifascist group, www.rechtsum.de. This exhibit, which was titled "Ausstellung rechts und ab durch die Mitte," was predicated on the assumption that the German Right goes through the center—and even into the conventional left.

27. Fauquet, "Berlioz au Panthéon?" *Le Monde,* February 9, 2000, and June 21, 2000.

must be faced in view of Mussolini's success of the 1920s. Similar admonitions are frequently expressed in the European and American establishment press about anything that appeals to the politics of nostalgia. Unless controlled, such fondness for the past could lead away from a multicultural path into what French journalist Bernard-Henri Lévy has called the pernicious "precincts of nationalist ideology."[28]

Those who are secure in their pure intentions also understand the pervasive evil of their Euro-American or German identity. It is something that must be devalued and eventually removed from human relations, in the transition to a global society that will "enrich" the Western world by replacing it. A useful precedent was the Allied "reeducation" of Germany after World War II, which proceeded from the premise that German political culture had to be radically reconstructed. Since the German past was soaked in "Prussian militarism," according to the Allies' Potsdam declaration in July 1945, it was best that the conquerors impose a new "constitutional patriotism."[29] In Western Europe the self-acknowledged pure of heart are now introducing their own civic culture, for which they are finding allies in the judiciary and civil service. So far, multiculturalism has mandated laws against "crimes of opinion," for the use of public education to socialize, and for the preferential treatment of Third World settlers, including tax support for Islamic institutions in numerical proportions exceeding what is allowed for the majority Christian religion.

■ Tolerance and Intolerance

Tolerance, understood as glorifying the foreign and the anti-Western, is different from courtesy to strangers. It is an expression of ancestral self-rejection, like the zeal of those Romans who upon joining the early church turned against their pagan heritage entirely. Although Christianity came to terms eventually with the

28. Lévy, *L'idéologie française*, 263.
29. This and other documents intended to make German students aware of their painful national history are available in *Die deutsche Frage*, ed. Lower Saxon Central Office for Political Education (Hannover, 1982), 70.

imperial establishment, multicultural political religion may not make peace with what it fails to transform. Like Marxism, it mimics Christianity, to the point of adapting certain Christian core experiences. The Post-Marxist Left has its own version of *metanoia*, the conversionary experience of the repentant sinner, who is now awaiting the "end of History" as we have known it. Those converted to the new teaching try to reach out to the impenitent, but like Saint Augustine amid the heresies of fifth-century North Africa, they sometimes call in the magistrates against the heretics who are corrupting the community of faith.

The "great migrations" into Europe cause Italian novelist and philosopher Umberto Eco to vibrate with joyous expectation. Eco, who has asked European governments to suppress ethnocentric criticism, looks forward to "the ethnic reconstruction of the countries of destination, an inexhaustible changing of customs, the unstoppable hybridization which will statistically alter the color of skin, hair, and eyes of the population." A French sociologist and former Communist-turned-multicultural Socialist and advisor to former French president Mitterrand, Edgar Morin, celebrates the "chaos that is Europe." Europe will find its true identity by opening its gates to Third World populations, who will "help it cast out its fundamental principles" and push it toward "organizational-economic anarchy." But the question that Italian Socialist minister of immigration Margherita Boniver posed in 1991 remains to be decided: "Which type of integration [individual or communal] should we be aiming at in building a multiracial, multiethnic, and multireligious society?" The more moderate path, according to Alberto Carosa and Guido Vignelli in *L'invasione silenciosa*, would seem to be individual integration, which would allow for a minimal common denominator and lead into "a mingling of races" *(meticciazione)*. This is generally what the *Wall Street Journal*'s feature writer Tamar Jacoby has advocated for the United States: high levels of Third World integration combined with the indoctrination of the newcomers in a specifically American creed. Although an affirmation of the pluralistic status quo and its "human rights" ideology, the socialization proposed would nurture American loyalty in a mounting immigrant population. The U.S. regime would provide the vehicle for implementing this globalist ideology and would receive in return the support of its citizens.[30]

In Europe, however, the Post-Marxist Left generally favors a more daring path, the leap into chaos that has proved so compelling for Morin and Eco. This is not only the preferred path of the political Left but also one that Christian churches have embraced more and more. In *Multiculturalism and the Politics of Guilt*, I examined the transposition of Christian symbols and doctrines in liberal Protestantism into a multicultural religion of guilt and penance. What is taken to be secularism is different from the mere removal of religious doctrines. It exists in relation to a post-Christian political religion that borrows from what it replaces. Occasionally the replacement looks sufficiently like the real article so that it can slip into and assume its identity. Carosa and Vignelli demonstrate the effects of this substitution in Italian Catholicism. An often amorphous guilt over past acts of intolerance and over material inequalities, an association of Third World cultures and religions with the "suffering just," a reduction of quintessential Christianity to equality and universality, and an expectation of living in some multicultural end-time all fuel the Catholic campaign for inclusiveness. Thus in a manifesto of the Catholic philanthropic organization Caritas published in 1996, we are told: "Immigration is a sign of a civilization called to bring together identity and universality, difference and equality. The diversity of cultures, ethnicities, and faiths is a source of social vitality that should be accepted and enjoyed by all Europeans inasmuch as it enriches our lives, our ideas, our creativity, and our political

30. Umberto Eco, "Quando l'Europa diventerà afro-europea," *L'Espresso* 1 (1990), 194; Edgar Morin, *Penser l'Europe* (Paris: Folio-Actuel, 1987), 24; *Il Manifesto*, May 1, 1991, 1; Alberto Carosa and Guido Vignelli, *L'invasione silenciosa: L'immigrazionnismo: Risorsa o complotto?* (Rome: Il Minotauro, 2002), 106–9; Tamar Jacoby, *Reinventing the Melting Pot: The New Americans and What It Means to Be American* (New York: Basic Books, 2004); see also John J. Miller, *The Unmaking of Americans: How Multiculturalism Has Undermined America's Assimilation Ethic* (New York: Free Press, 1998). This reference should not be mistaken for support for the creedal formulations these journalists are hoping to impose on the Third World immigrants whom they are happy to see immigrate. But what distinguishes their approach from the Post-Marxist one is at least minimal awareness of the social and cultural problems that may arise from multicultural politics.

world."[31] In a similar way, Archbishop Martini of Milan explained in 1990 that "the migratory process from the poorer South to the richer North is a great ethical and civil occasion for renewal and for inverting the course of decadence in Western European consumerism. The West should transform the reception of these immigrants into a racial, cultural, and religious integration that favors in Europe the emergence of a multiracial and multicultural society." Roger Cardinal Etchegaray, chairman of the Pontifical Council for Peace and Justice, goes beyond Martini in expressing his enthusiasm for the transmigration of Third World populations into his continent: "Now that the European community is about to open its frontiers, it would be foolish if it transformed itself into a comfortable fortress in the face of immigrants and refugees who are pressing in from the South and the East." The occasion was at hand to redistribute income and to turn the "shock of cultures and the mixing of cultures" into "epochal opportunity to attack the contradictions in which the entire society is stagnating."[32] Monsignor Giovanni Cheli of the Pontifical Council for Immigrants rejoices over another aspect of this mixing. In the end it will bring about a "society that is less nationalistic and in which all individuals are subject to rights." Immigration will culminate in "the reconciliation of once-distant peoples" as they are brought into contact. Or, as the World Vatican Conference on Immigration in 1991 expressed with eschatological hope, "Immigration represents the privileged point for the declaration and human promotion of solidarity."[33]

It may be helpful to raise and examine two objections to the critical observations presented. Church leaders, it might be said, are bowing to the inevitable when they applaud the increasing levels of Third World immigration into Italy (which is now approaching the legal figure of 250,000 each year). In any case some bishops may have interest in "evangelizing" the immigrants, which proves that they are not as devoted to a multireligious society as

---

31. *Avvenire*, November 19, 1996, 1.
32. C. M. Martini, *Relazione al terzo convegno del Pontificio Consiglio dei Migranti* (Rome: n.p., 1991), 8; Roger Etchegaray, "Solidarité pour les nouvelles migrations," in ibid., 7.
33. *Avvenire*, September 28, 1991, 1, and October 5, 1991, 1.

suggested by Carosa and Vignelli. The rub here is that Catholic leaders and organizations, most notably Caritas, have been in the vanguard of the proimmigration forces.[34] They have not been pulled along but have led. Their endorsement of a multicultural Western Europe includes support for the enriching experience of having non-Western religions. This means rejoicing publicly as Muslims come into their country, many of whom have no desire to be westernized, if that term still retains a definite meaning. Moreover, identifiably Catholic as well as Socialist politicians have worked toward giving Muslims parity with Christians in Italy and elsewhere in Europe. They have also provided funding for Muslim communal activities in Italian cities that has been taken from resources originally earmarked for Catholics.

My point is not to disparage the act of assisting the stranger, which may be a commendable Judeo-Christian virtue. Nor am I denying categorically the case-by-case consideration of allowing skilled laborers to cross national borders or entire continents for doing what countries cannot perform adequately with their own available workforce. What is being emphasized is the frenzied desire to repopulate the West with non-Western immigrants, some of whom are unmistakably hostile, and the propensity to exalt what is non-Western as a replacement for Western moral and spiritual impoverishment. Those who imagine that they have been inwardly transformed see this task as so vital that no opposition to it can be brooked. Committees for vigilance, and in Germany mass demonstrations of the antifascist "Revolt of the Decent," have been organized to expose and marginalize those who raise objections to the denationalization of their country.

In a dramatic act of spurning one's biological ancestors, antifascist activists, led by members of a group called Antideutsche, expressed vociferous support for the Allied bombing of Frankfurt and other German cities during World War II. While other Germans had gathered to mourn the deaths caused by the devastation of the Frankfurt inner city on March 22, 1944, the self-proclaimed

34. See Carosa and Vignelli, *L'invasione silenciosa*, 128–56; Marzio Barbagli, *Immigrazione e criminalità in Italia* (Bologna: Il Mulino, 1998); Comunità di Sant'Egidio, *Stranieri nostri fratelli: Verso una società multirazziale* (Brescia: Morcelliana, 1989); and the extended interview with political theorist and longtime social democrat Giovanni Sartori in *Il Giorno*, September 15, 2000, 1.

voices of German conscience screamed at the crowd: "they should have killed them all!"[35] This antinational crusade must supposedly go on until all Germans have been desensitized to their antecedents. The same rite of purification has caught on elsewhere in Europe—though not to the same masochistic degree. Although a "shock of cultures" belongs to Europe's future, according to Cardinal Martini, somehow that, too, will end well, once a new race and social type emerges out of the fitful ordeal of mixing. Never to be considered are these catastrophic scenarios: Islamicists wreaking havoc politically on a Western world where they have settled but whose way of life they abhor; other, non-Western cultures and their bearers, who have a deeper sense of identity than Westerners, imposing *their* values eventually; and the violence that Third World populations have caused to escalate in Europe continuing to increase. Such anxieties are not permissible to the extent that the multiculturalists burn with a post-Christian faith in their amalgamating mission.

A final observation concerns the Post-Marxist Left's attraction to how Communism worked in practice—and not as an abstract human goal. Despite the differences between European Communist governments and European multiculturalists, the European Left happily papers over Communist crimes and blames those who mention them as apologists for the far Right. Why, might we ask, are they laboring to defend a brutal heritage from which the current Left might do well to cut itself loose? Among other reasons to be noted would be the value of the Communist experiment as a prototypical Christian heresy and would-be Christian successor. Like the Post-Marxist Left, Communists were at war with bourgeois civilization, while pursuing a universalist, egalitarian vision.

Yet this conscious break from the cultural past was not as true for Communists of an earlier generation as it is for the current Left. It is hard to imagine the leaders of the former Soviet Union celebrating homosexual lifestyles or throwing open their societies to Islamicists. The German Democratic Republic made Luther

35. See Werner Olles's commentary on the demonstration against the memorial vigil in Frankfurt commemorating the bombing of the city in *Junge Freiheit*, April 2, 2004, 6.

and Frederick the Great into forerunners of its Marxist regime, while West German journalists, academics, and politicians presented these and other German historical figures as contributors to the Nazi catastrophe.[36] Despite the affinity of some West German Social Democrats for the East German Communist government, it was not the Marxists in the East but the West German progressives who sought to overcome the German past by treating it as a prelude to the Third Reich. It was the West Germans, not the East German Communists, who insisted on the "exclusive blame" of Germany for World War I as well as World War II. Communists inside and outside of Germany viewed World War I as a battle among competing capitalist nations. Not Communism but its successor on the left has taken over Susan Sontag's assessment of the West as the "cancer of humanity."[37] And in the German case, this Left has applied self-denigrating judgments to its nation with righteous delight. But, equally important, those who express this collective self-hatred invariably exclude themselves from the indictment. It is they who can rise above the cult of guilt by embracing it and by pointing to a future totally unlike the past.

The Post-Marxist Left goes beyond the totalitarian movements of the past, provocatively analyzed by Voegelin and Hannah Arendt, in emphatically rejecting the Western cultural and historical heritage. It has exerted journalistic, judicial, and bureaucratic force to destroy any self-affirming Western consciousness and European national identity. Although politically less violent than other Lefts, it is culturally and socially more radical. It has also faced less overt resistance than earlier, more brutal political religions. Its present success may be partly attributed to a misrepresentation of what is going on. In a work that sold over three hundred thousand copies, *Left and Right: The Significance of a Political Distinction*, Italian Socialist senator and longtime political theorist Norberto Bobbio defends the continued use of left-right distinctions after the fall of the Soviet empire.[38] According to Bobbio, such traditional

36. See Paul Gottfried, "Über den deutschen Nachkriegskonservatismus," *Criticon*, 89 (May/June 1985), 112–13.

37. This memorable phrase from Susan Sontag's essays of the 1960s can be found in the *Columbia World of Quotations* (1996), 57412.

38. Norberto Bobbio, *Left and Right: The Significance of a Political Distinction*, trans. Allan Cameron (Chicago: University of Chicago Press, 1997).

nomenclature continues to have value, inasmuch as there are still rival partisans who stand behind the two opposing principles of equality and inequality. Therefore, "left and right" still function as operative labels for distinctive ideological camps that in their moderate forms sustain parliamentary governments. What has ceased to matter for the Left, according to Bobbio, is "antifascist militancy," a position that he associates with a Communist-controlled, pro-Soviet Left. Little did this author sense, at the time that his book saw light in 1994, that antifascism was coming to define the Post-Marxist Left. Whether this will remain the case indefinitely is open to question; nonetheless, in the short and middle terms, the European Left will not likely abandon multiculturalism—or forsake the antifascism that is now synonymous with it.

CONCLUSION

THE POST-MARXIST Left grew out of circumstances treated both in these pages and in my earlier works, dealing with the end of the liberal era and with mass democracy and multiculturalism. The developments analyzed arose from the weakening of a bourgeois liberal society and from its replacement by administered democracy. The consolidation of a managerial state, appealing to the ideal of service to the people and to "scientific" governance, sealed the doom of the society it took over. The new regime appropriated the functions of the Victorian family, mediated relations between parents and children and between contending spouses, and eventually came to preside over a society of deracinated and footloose consumers. The willingness of American churches to go along with these progressive changes caused their own institutional marginalization and made the transition to a new order easier, by removing what might have been a source of cultural friction. Indeed the triumph of multiculturalism, as a political ideology, received impetus from transformed Christian denominations, and, contrary to a mistaken impression that my book on multiculturalism might have generated, has been as strong in the Catholic Church as it has been among Protestant denominations.[1]

The Post-Marxist Left represents politics in a more radical key, one in which traditional class loyalties, be it to the bourgeoisie

1. See the summarizing of my studies by Eric Cox, "Empire of Compassion," in *American Outlook* (winter 2004): 55–57.

or to the working class, have disintegrated. This radicalization occurred as the working class lost its distinctive features in a largely postindustrial society and because of the relentless inroads of managerial democracy. The staffing of such government by a postliberal elite has accelerated the movement toward a new political culture. In this culture, administrators, operating in conjunction with the media and judiciary, have gone from providing social services into supporting postbourgeois and postproletariat lifestyles and attitudes. This elite and its allies have forged a leftist ideology that is no longer Marxist but has imposed its own form of sacral politics.

Curiously, the advocates of this Post-Marxist ideology have also hastened to assume the baggage of the Communist past. Because of its opposition to bourgeois civilization and a view of itself as standing in the line of a long-lived leftist tradition, the Post-Marxist Left in Europe continues to defend or to exculpate the Communist record of tyranny. The recasting of today's political confrontations as reenactments of the Left's battles of the 1930s is based on questionable parallels but does furnish the appearance of continuity for the European Left's vision of itself. And the Post-Marxist Left's successful presentation of "fascism" as the past that never passes makes its denial or avoidance of the record of the Communists in power work in the court of public opinion. It is never appropriate, or so we are made to believe, to delve with excessive zeal into Communist misbehavior, when Nazi or fascist threats are still omnipresent. The best approach to this threat is seen as having administrative "professionals" educate the public in "tolerance," while judges and the police work to isolate the offending bigots.

While in the sixties Max Horkheimer stated the view that the present age reveals a "narrowing of rationality," this narrowing has affected the spectrum of permissible political differences even more than philosophical thought. In *After Liberalism*, the argument is made that mass democratic political debate depends on the less and less substantive distinctions between rival social democratic camps. It is a hyped-up disagreement over policy issues that are to be implemented by state administrators: how to tax citizens for socialized medicine, which taxing system will yield the most revenue while affecting investment in the private sector the least, or whether to raise the national minimum wage. In the world of the

Post-Marxist Left, sweeping social change has overtaken the traditional Left as much as it has the now stigmatized Right. The working-class consciousness that had marked the socialist past, and was connected sociologically to profoundly conservative attitudes, has ceased to count. This once established leftist consciousness has yielded to a multicultural Left, built on the domination of state functionaries, lifestyle innovators, and those who favor a Third World resettlement of the West.

Although it may be too early to know where any of this will lead, presumably history will not go into reverse. The social preconditions for a return to the past even in a limited sense, such as going back to the gender roles and constitutionally more limited welfare state of the mid-twentieth century, are no longer present. And the reason is not simply technological change. Those who have controlled society politically and have worked in harmony with educators and mediacrats have altered social morality. Even more significantly, they have imposed themselves everywhere, invariably in the name of "liberating" oppressed individuals from their families and by now shattered communities. They have transformed consciousness and, given the influx of non-Western populations and religions and the declining birthrate of the more indigenous Europeans, there is no compelling reason to think this situation will change.

Nor does it seem possible or even remotely convincing that Europeans can counter the Post-Marxist Left by reading or lecturing about "values." Even those moral preferences that have the judgment of the ages behind them will only work to the extent that they are institutionally grounded and wedded to a structure of authority. Conservative values are those that maintain and justify such authority, but in our time they may also be those that legitimate governments that are plunging headlong into multicultural experimentation. Expressing respect for authority or "institutions" or devising arguments to sanctify the status quo is not enough to alter the historical situation, one built on programmed changes that do not allow for serious opposition. And unless a rising or dominant elite would spearhead a campaign against the multicultural agenda, which is the sacred commitment of the Post-Marxist Left and its American counterparts, it is hard to see how such a purpose can be achieved. Talking about values or the "vision thing" among the established political parties is to raise the issue of electoral strategy—and nothing more. And those parties that think outside the box will suffer judicial condemnation and be pushed into illegality, as recently happened to the Vlaams Blok, a regionalist party in Belgium that opposes the immigration of Third World Muslims into Flemish cities.

Perhaps it is neither "value-education" nor philosophical rationality but what remains of class identity, whether aristocratic, bourgeois, or working-class, that is the greatest obstacle to socialization by the postmodern state. Both inherited social roles and the accompanying behavioral models render problematic the inculcation of contemporary state-enforced creeds.[2] It is hard to recode bureaucratically those who have learned to think and act as members of a functioning stratified society. This conviction led me into a softer view of those rank-and-file French and Italian Communists who were voting during the middle of the twentieth century. Unlike those emotionally troubled intellectuals who tried to join them, these voters felt solidarity with other members of the working class. And though this solidarity included *la bugia grande* (the big lie) when it came to justifying Soviet behavior, the European working class has not been the only group to view Communist dictatorships indulgently. The current European Left is doing the same, despite better formal education and far more disposable wealth. Moreover, this current Left includes socialists who belong to parties that once readily acknowledged the Soviet threat to Western freedom.

The Communist working-class electorate, as depicted by Kriegel and Ragusa, were for the most part family wage earners. They were people loyal to their kin as well as to other workers and supported

2. For a critical but fair treatment of my social contextualization of values, which have been described as Marxism leaning right, see W. Wesley McDonald's *Russell Kirk and the Age of Ideology* (Columbia: University of Missouri Press, 2004), 209–12; see also Claes G. Ryn and Paul Gottfried, "Dialogue on Power," *Humanitas* 14, no. 1 (2001), 96–107; Germana Paraboschi's exploration of the struggle to introduce a historicist perspective on the American intellectual right in *Leo Strauss e la Destra americana* (Rome: Riuniti, 1992); and Virgil Nemoianu's survey of like interpretations in recent European social thought, "Changes in Europe," *Modern Age* 46, nos. 1–2 (winter/spring 2004): 32–42.

a party they imagined, whatever else that party claimed to be, would improve their material situation.[3] They were not engaged in a moral revolution designed to satisfy their individual cravings— and did not generally hope to use the government as a battering ram against the bourgeois family. Although CP pamphlets did stress the need to liberate women from the kitchen and church pews, these rhetorical appeals did not likely account for the party's mass support. Communist voters were radical redistributionists but also resembled that blue-collar class portrayed by social commentator Christopher Lasch in his defenses of American populism. Lasch presented his embodiments of working-class decency, particularly in his last work, *Revolt of the Elites,* as the popular counterweight to a new class of international self-indulged hedonists flaunting wealth and outrageous lifestyles. Lasch's sketch of a rebellious elite is drawn with overly broad strokes while his populist heroes seem to have been lifted out of a 1950s Catholic ethnic community. But the polarity his work features does correspond to a relevant social reality.[4] He is offering an idealized picture of the European working-class Left while furnishing a generally accurate depiction of the Post-Marxist Left. What Lasch excludes from the second picture, however, is something central to our discussion, namely, the post-Christian religious fervor of the post-Communist Left. It is not merely dislike for bourgeois society mixed with erotic fantasy but a deep dedication to historical and anthropological transformation that drives this Left. Without bemoaning the passing of an erstwhile European leftist voter, it might be possible to note how little, relatively speaking, he desired. And it might be justified to wonder whether his successor, a lifestyle radical equipped with a bulging stock portfolio, has favored the rise of a less revolutionary Left.

The attempt to trace this leftist type to a distinctively American culture may be the least digestible part of the argument of this book, and it is one that both America boosters and European leftists will reject with equal outrage. At one point in the not dis-

3. For sympathetic studies of the *communistes de troupe,* see Georges Lavau, *A quoi sert le Parti C.F.?* (Paris: Fayard, 1981); and J.-P. Molinari, *Les ouvriers communistes: Sociologie de l'adhésion ouvrière au PC* (Paris: L'Harmatton, 1990).

4. Christopher Lasch, *Revolt of the Elites and the Betrayal of Democracy* (New York: Norton, 1995).

tant past, European observers saw the decisive role played by the American presence on European life as an indisputable fact. Whether they liked or feared that presence, they never denied it was there. Nor did they waste their time inventing distinctions between early American feminism, gay rights, and diversity and those forms of these tendencies Europeans took over and sharpened. In the past Europeans were so terrified by American ideas or "reeducation" that the most conservative of them sometimes seemed afraid of American influence more than of Soviet arms. (Note the criticism then was not that the United States was insufficiently multicultural but that it was subverting the European heritage.)

German sociologist Arnold Gehlen expressed these anxieties in the sixties and early seventies, as he looked at his people's moral and cultural frailties. Unlike the Soviet bloc, the United States, reasoned Gehlen, a staunch anti-Communist old-fashioned German liberal, posed a continuing temptation for Germany's rising generation, which had become contemptuous of the national past and infatuated by everything American: "In Germany one sees the scrupulous absorption of American manners, illusions, defense mechanisms, *Playboy* and drug culture, and open enrollment in higher education, for here no less than there the intellectuals are directing the destinies of the countries more than anywhere else. Nonetheless, what we lack are the American reserves in national energy and self-confidence, primitiveness and generosity, wealth and potential of every kind. With our beaten-down history and our youth seduced by volatile phrases, with a top-heavy industry, which is international in its character, nothing can keep us from losing our national identity."[5]

Gehlen views as an equally perilous American import for his countrymen the fusion of ideas about progress and secularization. American intellectuals and journalists were in the forefront of a fashion that Germans were then happily absorbing, treating progress as a cultural force to be advanced through the formation of a post-Christian social consciousness. Gehlen does not see this tendency as being specifically German. What he was investigating is

5. See Arnold Gehlen, *Einblicke* (Frankfurt am Main: Vittorio Klostermann, 1972), 113–14.

a form of cultural radicalism exported from Germany, remolded in America, and then sent back to Europe. At the same time, he observes, sociopolitical patterns will not likely be altered, particularly the movement toward a "total system including state and society," "a union of production and welfare in which the increase of economic performance and the guarantee of welfare and social insurance form the overriding imperative."[6] Although Gehlen ignores the tendency of public administration to sap economic productivity, he was correct, in 1971, about managerial states putting themselves in charge of mixed economies. What intellectuals would change in the new order, partly on the basis of American ideas, was not its material substructure but its ideological component.

But this happened in a way in which the generally perceptive Gehlen did not foresee. Contrary to his beliefs that it was "die Intelligenz," but not "workers, employers, and state bureaucrats," who embraced "democratization in an extreme form," the new egalitarian ideology affected precisely those who were supposed to resist it. "Democratization" became primarily a cultural imperative while the "total system" would be directed toward creating a postbourgeois society and culture. By now that incentive to social engineering has gone from the Old to the New World and then back again and in the process altered Europe even more dramatically than us.

---

6. Ibid., 26–27. For observations about former Communist societies stressing their premodern continuities, see William Mills, *Black Sea Sketches* (Rockford, Ill.: Chronicles Press, 2003).

INDEX